Wolves

LIFE IN THE PACK

Wolves

LIFE IN THE PACK

CHRIS WHITT

BARNES &NOBLE BOOKS

NEW YORK

A BARNES & NOBLE BOOK

©2003 by Barnes & Noble Publishing, Inc.

ISBN 0-7607-4683-4

Editor: Susan Lauzau
Art Director: Jeff Batzli
Designer: Midori Nakamura
Photography Editor: Lori Epstein
Production Manager:
Karen Matsu Greenberg

Color separations by
Fine Arts Repro House Co., Ltd.
Printed in Belgium by
PROOST NV

1 3 5 7 9 10 8 6 4 2

CONTENTS

CHAPTER ONE
Introducing Wolves . . . . page 6

CHAPTER TWO
Living in Wolf Society . . . . page 44

CHAPTER THREE
Hunting: A Group Effort . . . . page 74

CHAPTER FOUR
Wolves: The Next Generation . . . . page 100

CHAPTER FIVE
Humans and Wolves . . . . page 124

RESOURCES . . . . page 142

INDEX . . . . page 143

CHAPTER ONE

INTRODUCING WOLVES

Introducing Wolves

A compelling creature of beauty and mystery, the wolf has long fascinated its human neighbors, who have, over time, admired this magnificent predator for its superb hunting skills, feared and reviled the wild wolf as a threat to both people and livestock, and ultimately come to recognize it as an untamed presence worth preserving. Humans and wolves have historically traveled together over much of the same territory, both species adapting themselves admirably to the varied terrain and different prey available across the northern hemisphere. At some point in the ancient past, by about fifteen thousand years ago and perhaps long before, the two creatures attached themselves to each other as faithful companions, and the dog, directly descended from the wolf, became the first domesticated animal.

But even after the dog settled into the embrace of the human community, its wild relatives continued to roam untamed, eventually becoming the most widespread and successful wild canid on the planet. As the human population increased dramatically in the late eighteenth and throughout the nineteenth century, people encroached on wild wolves' territory more aggressively than ever before. With this increased contact came the perception that wild wolves posed a grave danger to human society. Predictably, people sought to systematically eliminate this threat, and by the early twentieth century had pushed the wolf in North America almost to the brink of extinction.

After thirty years on the endangered species list and a heroic effort on the part of conservationists, wolves have been successfully reintroduced in parts of the United States and Canada. Today populations of these magnificent predators have recovered to the point that the federal government has down-listed them from "endangered" to "threatened" status in some states.

MAN'S BEST FRIEND

ABOVE: An Alaskan malamute bears an uncanny resemblance to a wolf, partly a product of genetic heritage and—after the dog was domesticated—partly a response to the same frigid environment.

OPPOSITE: All dogs, no matter how different they may be in size and physical appearance, belong to the species *Canis familiaris*, and all trace their ancestry back to the wolf.

According to recent genetic studies, dogs evolved directly from wolves rather than from jackals or coyotes, as some scientists had previously supposed. But researchers disagree about the date by which dogs were domesticated and about when the process began.

Based on the archaeological record, many scientists believe that domestic dogs date back approximately fifteen thousand years. A jawbone from Germany that is approximately fourteen thousand years old and the twelve-thousand-year-old bones of a pup found in Israel provide the earliest sound archaeological evidence of domestic dogs, but researchers working with genetic data are convinced that the dog's origins are much older, and that concrete archaeological evidence of these earlier origins may be either lost or as yet undiscovered.

Molecular genetic techniques allow researchers to extrapolate based on the mutation rate in certain DNA sequences. The genetic diversity in the markers studied indicates a much earlier domestication date for dogs than the fifteen thousand years previously estimated.

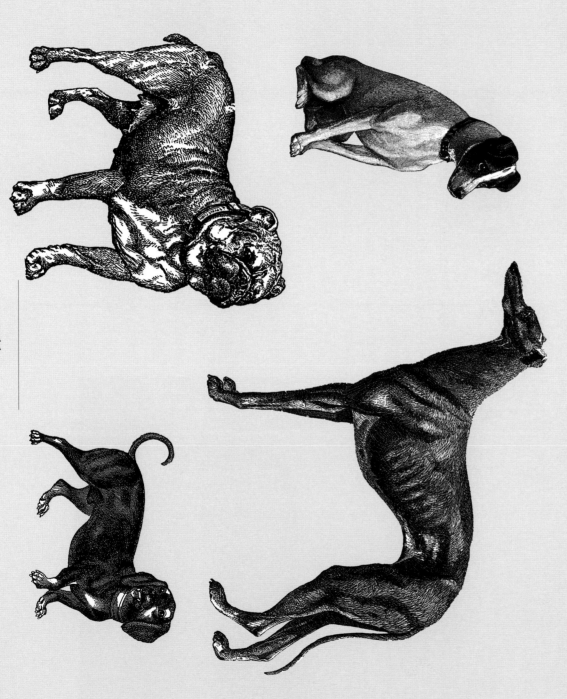

because the number of mutations identified could not have occurred in that relatively short period of time. But the calculations involved in these extrapolations are inexact so a precise date for the divergence of dogs and wolves is difficult to estimate. Current genetic research estimates that the date may be anywhere from forty thousand to one hundred thousand years ago, much earlier than scientists had previously thought.

The reasons that some ancient wolves chose to associate themselves with humans and the early mechanisms for domestication are likewise widely debated. One theory posits that hunter-gatherers may have adopted motherless wolf pups, raising them as pets and habituating them to humans in the process. Others suggest that wolves began to hang around human camps voluntarily, drawn by the scrap heaps that inevitably piled up. However the relationship began, it clearly proved mutually

beneficial, as wolves secured a reliable source of food and shelter and humans gained an effective garbage disposal as well as a companion and watch animal.

Wolves' natural social structure left them predisposed to accept authority, and they readily replaced the leader of the wolf pack with a human master. Over time, as it became apparent that wolves produced pups that shared the traits of their parents, people began to understand the basic concepts of breeding, and selected for traits that would serve them well. Hunting, herding, and retrieving are all skills that were eventually enhanced by selective breeding, and as travel among human populations increased, dogs with useful characteristics were no doubt traded to other peoples.

Those ancient wolves, for their part, had embarked on a course that would change both canine and human history forever, becoming in the process man's best and most valued friend.

11

Meet the Canid Family

Wolves are part of the family called Canidae, which consists of thirty-five different species, including coyotes, foxes, jackals, dingoes, dholes, and wild and domestic dogs. The most doglike of these animals—coyotes, wolves, dingoes, and the like—are classified together in the genus *Canis*, while foxes fall into the genus *Vulpes*. Animals in the genus *Canis* are all referred to as canines (though we often think of this word as applying exclusively to domestic dogs), and share a number of distinguishing characteristics. Among these distinctive features are non-retractable claws and four-toed paws, with a dew claw (a residual fifth toe) on each of the front paws.

All canines have forty-two teeth, and most have relatively long muzzles and long, slender legs. They also typically have thick coats and bushy tails, with scent glands located at the base of their tails. While many in the canid family are social creatures, depending on other members of the pack for successful hunting, some—most notably foxes—are chiefly solitary, and prey mainly on rodents, birds, and rabbits or hares.

A Look at Wolf Taxonomy

Taxonomy, the science of naming and classifying plants and animals according to their natural relationships to one another, has evolved over time and continues to shift in response to researchers' ever-changing body of knowledge about their subjects. As new genetic information becomes available, biologists are able to reclassify animals and plants based on their deeper genetic relationships rather than purely on their superficial physical similarities and differences or on their geographical distribution.

Despite scientific advances that allow us to clarify specific classifications, the basic structure of the original classifying system—developed by Swedish physician and botanist Carolus Linnaeus in the eighteenth century—still survives today. It shows the groups to which an animal belongs, from the most general to the most specific. The following chart examines the taxonomy of the eastern gray wolf, *Canis lupus lycaon*.

BELOW: The wolf is the largest member of the dog family and shares many characteristics with domestic dogs, however the wolf is distinguished by longer legs and larger paws than even the most wolflike breeds. It is also more social than any other canid, spending most of its life in the company of other wolves.

Kingdom	Animalia	Multicellular organisms that do not have cell walls and cannot make food via photosynthesis
Phylum	Chordata	Animals that have backbones or other internal support
Class	Mammalia	Chordates that have fur and produce milk
Order	Carnivora	Mammals that subsist chiefly on meat
Family	Canidae	Carnivores that share distinguishing doglike traits, such as 42 teeth, long muzzles, and scent glands at their tails
Genus	*Canis*	Wolves, coyotes, jackals, dingoes, and dogs
Species	*lupus*	Gray wolf
Subspecies	*lycaon*	Eastern gray wolf

At one time, as many as twenty-four wolf subspecies were believed to populate North America, but most of these have recently been reclassified into just five subspecies: *arctos*, the Arctic wolf; *lycaon*, the Eastern gray wolf; *nubilus*, the Great Plains wolf; *baileyi*, the Mexican wolf; and *occidentalis*, the Rocky Mountain wolf. Among the characteristics that distinguish the different subspecies are fur color, size, and the shape of the skull. Despite the fact that each subspecies possesses particular physical characteristics, some individuals may be difficult, if not impossible, to classify into a particular recognized subspecies because the ranges of subspecies may overlap and wolves commonly interbreed. Thus, wolves in those zones where ranges overlap may feature characteristics of two different subspecies.

There is also speculation that the red wolf (*Canis rufus*), the other wolf species of North America, is actually a subspecies of the gray wolf or perhaps a hybrid of the gray wolf and its close cousin the coyote (*Canis latrans*).

BELOW: Most biologists agree that the red wolf is a species separate from the gray wolf, but some researchers maintain that it should properly be classified a subspecies of *Canis lupus*. Interbreeding between red wolves and coyotes has only made defining the parameters of the species more difficult, as many animals remaining in the traditional red wolf range are actually hybrids.

WHAT'S IN A SUBSPECIES?

Gray wolf subspecies share the traits common to all wolves, including strong social bonds, cooperative hunting, vocal communication, and a territorial nature. However, different subspecies do have some characteristics that make them distinct, chiefly their physical appearance and their home range. Some subspecies have larger territories and/or smaller pack and litter sizes, and this is often a function of the availability of prey in the region in which the wolves are living.

ARCTIC WOLF
(Canis lupus arctos)

Arctic wolves live chiefly above sixty-seven degrees north latitude, in a region covered for much of the year by snow and ice, and they are supremely adapted for their surroundings. Their thick white fur both camouflages them in their snow-covered environs and keeps them warm in temperatures that can dip to seventy degrees below zero (-21°C). They also have shorter muzzles and legs, and smaller ears than other gray wolves. Because the ground in the Arctic is frozen for most of the year, Arctic wolves often make their dens in caves, along outcroppings, or in shallow depressions rather than digging a den in the earth. Arctic wolves prey mainly on musk oxen, Arctic hares, caribou, ptarmigans, seals, and birds.

BELOW: Arctic wolf

ABOVE: Eastern gray wolf

EASTERN GRAY WOLF
(Canis lupus lycaon)
A.K.A.: Eastern timber wolf

The Eastern gray wolf was the first subspecies in North America to be recognized as distinct, in 1775, and it originally had the largest range of all the wolf subspecies in the New World. These wolves are physically distinct from other North American gray wolves, with grizzled brownish coats and lighter tan fur around their ears, though some individuals may be black or white. While they previously ranged throughout the northeastern United States as well as southeastern Canada, they are now confined mainly to densely forested or legally protected areas of their former range.

GREAT PLAINS WOLF
(Canis lupus nubilus)
A.K.A.: buffalo wolf

This gray wolf subspecies is the one now most commonly found in the United States, and has a coat of grizzled gray, black, or buff. The Great Plains wolf preys mainly on white-tailed deer, moose, beaver, snowshoe hares, and small mammals and birds; in the past, buffalo were among the prey animals of the Great Plains wolf. It formerly ranged throughout the United States and into southern Canada, but with the decimation of the buffalo and the systematic eradication of wolves in the late nineteenth and early twentieth centuries, the Great Plains wolf was eliminated in much of its range. It survived in small populations in the western Great Lakes region, and today the population has recovered in some states to the point that this wolf is listed as threatened rather than endangered, and is a candidate for complete removal from the endangered species list in some areas.

Mexican Wolf
(Canis lupus baileyi)
A.K.A.: lobo

The Mexican wolf, the smallest North American wolf, is the most genetically distinct subspecies. Its coat is a grizzled buff and salt-and-pepper gray, mixed with some red. This wolf originally ranged throughout Mexico and into the American Southwest, where it traditionally preyed upon white-tailed deer, mule deer, elk, javelina, rabbits, and other small animals. The Mexican wolf is currently endangered; it has been reintroduced to the wild, in small numbers, in Arizona.

BELOW: Mexican wolf

ABOVE: Rocky Mountain wolf

Rocky Mountain Wolf
(Canis lupus occidentalis)
A.K.A.: Mackenzie Valley wolf; Alaskan wolf

The Rocky Mountain wolf is the largest wolf subspecies native to North America, and has a coat of gray, black, white, or tan. It typically preys on bison, elk, moose, caribou, Dall sheep, Sitka black-tailed deer, mountain goats, beaver, salmon, vole, ground squirrels, and snowshoe hares. This subspecies is perhaps best known as the wolf reintroduced to Yellowstone National Park and to areas in Idaho. Its historic range encompassed Alaska and western Canada, including the Aleutian Islands. This subspecies is no longer considered endangered.

How Wolves Came to Be

Ironically enough, wolves and their chief prey, ungulates such as deer and moose, have an ancestor in common on the family tree. These early mammals developed the ability to run long distances as well as a relatively high level of intelligence, traits that both wolves and ungulates share today. During the Late Cretaceous period, approximately sixty-four to sixty-five million years ago, mammals began to specialize, filling distinct ecological niches that had been left open by the mass extinction of dinosaurs.

Out of this specialization came a carnivorous order of mammals, called Carnivora, in the Early Paleocene epoch, some sixty-three million years ago. These meat-eaters, from which all modern carnivores are descended, had large brains and sharp, flesh-tearing teeth called carnassials. Further specialization resulted in the Miacidae, a family in the order Carnivora. *Miacis* was a small, tree-climbing animal with a slender, weasel-like body and a long, thick tail. All members of the dog family are descended from *Miacis*, as are bears, cats, civets, hyenas, raccoons, weasels, mongooses, seals, sea lions, and walruses.

RIGHT: *Miacis*, a short-limbed, weasellike creature, walked the earth about fifty million years ago. From this small, intelligent carnivore evolved wolves and other members of the dog family as well as other meat-eaters like bears and raccoons.

It was during the Early Oligocene, roughly thirty-seven million years ago, that *Hesperocyon*, the first canid genus, appeared in North America. *Hesperocyon* walked on its toes and had the long muzzle and characteristic forty-two teeth of modern canids. Most animals within *Hesperocyon* died out, but the foxlike *Leptocyon* branch led during the Late Miocene, around ten million years ago, to three genera: *Urocyon* and *Vulpes* (both fox genera), and the familiar *Canis*, which today includes wolves, domestic dogs, jackals, coyotes, and dingoes. Despite the appearance of the genus *Canis*, the gray wolf species, *Canis lupus*, would not arise for another nine million years.

Around eight million years ago, small coyote-like dogs crossed the Bering Land bridge from North America into Eurasia, and began to distribute canid relatives across Asia, into western Europe, and eventually to Africa and South America. The fossil record shows that by the Early Pleistocene, approximately four to five million years ago, several identifiable wolf species had appeared in Europe and North America. During the Pleistocene, the repeated emergence and disappearance of an icy bridge across the Bering Strait, created by cycles of glaciation and rising and falling sea levels, allowed animals to alternately travel back and forth between the continents of North America and Eurasia, and then become stranded by the waters of the Bering Strait.

By about three hundred thousand years ago, in the Late Pleistocene, modern wolves, *Canis lupus*, had fully evolved in Eurasia. They crossed the Bering land bridge and populated North America, where they encountered the legendary dire wolf (*Canis dirus*). The dire wolf was a massive predator, much larger and more robust than the gray wolf, with powerful jaws and huge teeth. More than two thousand of these formidable animals were unearthed from the La Brea tar pits, in California, where they had ventured to feed on other animals mired there and become stuck themselves. While dire wolves became extinct at the end of the last ice age, gray wolves survived and thrived as the largest canine predator left on earth.

Red wolves have a murky evolutionary history, which mirrors their ambiguous status as a species. Some scientists argue that the red wolf (*Canis rufus*) is actually a hybrid of the gray wolf and the coyote. Others contend that the red wolf is a species of wolf native to North America, and was outcompeted by the larger gray wolf and forced into a relatively small range. Many acknowledge that, whatever the red wolf's original genetic makeup, today's red wolves have most likely interbred over the years with coyotes, a necessity caused by the dearth of red wolf mates due to extermination by humans.

ABOVE: As predators that evolved to hunt large, swift herd animals, wolves are well adapted to running long distances. This black phase animal—caught by the camera in midair—shows the long, graceful stride of the wolf, an important advantage in its fight for survival.

The Gray Wolf

Christened *Canis lupus* in 1758 by Linnaeus, the gray wolf is also popularly known as the timber wolf, tundra wolf, or silver wolf. The largest member of the canid family, the male gray wolf can grow to as much as six and a half feet (2m) in length (nose tip to tail tip), and stands from twenty-six (66cm) to thirty-two (81.3cm) inches high at the shoulder. Average weight for a male ranges from seventy to one hundred and ten pounds (154–242kg), with females generally a bit smaller, weighing in at fifty to eighty-five pounds (22.7–38.6kg) and reaching lengths up to six feet (1.8m) from the tip of the nose to the tip of the tail. Wolves in northern latitudes—in Canada, Alaska, and the Pacific Northwest region of the United States—tend to be larger than their counterparts in more southern areas, though this trend does not hold true of wolves living in the high Arctic; these wolves are somewhat smaller.

While the majority of "gray" wolves are indeed some shade of gray—or more likely a combination of fur colors that appears overall as pale to charcoal gray—many are pure white, dark black, tan, cream, reddish, brownish, or almost

BELOW: These black phase wolves look relaxed but watchful. The term "phase" refers to the permanent color of the animal's fur, which is determined by genetics, and does not mean that the wolf changes color with the seasons.

OPPOSITE: Arctic wolves look much like other wolves, but their fur is typically white or cream-colored, which helps to camouflage them in a snowy environment.

ABOVE: While a preponderance of wolves are gray, there is enormous variation in fur color throughout the species, and even wolves born into the same litter may have different pelt colors. Often, a wolf's coat is a mix of many different-colored hairs, which creates an overall impression of gray, with darker fur extending down the back and tail. Paler fur typically appears on the animal's belly, legs, ears, and snout.

OPPOSITE: Wolves possess several layers of fur, including coarse outer guard hairs that protect the animal from rain and snow, and fine soft underfur that keeps it warm even in subzero temperatures. Those animals living in the far north have particularly thick and luxurious fur. In the warmer months, they lose much of their insulating underfur.

21

immerable variations of these colors. A pup with one of these more "exotic" colors may be born to two wolves who are both gray, and littermates may be different in color. Each wolf coat is unique, with no exact matches of color and pattern the world over. In fact, coat markings are one of the ways that wolves can be distinguished from one another.

The hairs on a wolf's outer coat are multi-colored, sometimes with black, white, gray, and brown all appearing on the same hair shaft. Mixed together, these hairs of varying hues give the wolf's coat its singular grizzled look. Like people, wolves' hair turns gray as the animals grow older, and you can often pick out a relatively elderly wolf by the gray around its muzzle. Black wolves' coats likewise fade with the advancing years.

During the winter, a wolf's coat—which is composed of several layers of fur—grows thicker and more abundant. The topmost layer is made up of guard hairs—long, water-repellent hairs that serve to protect the wolf from rain and snow. Fur around the wolf's shoulders is exceptionally thick, and guard hairs in this area may grow up to five inches (12.7cm) long. Beneath the guard hairs is a dense layer of downy underfur, which insulates the wolf against the cold. Another type of insulation is provided by white hairs, which are hollow and allow air inside the shaft to warm the wolf further.

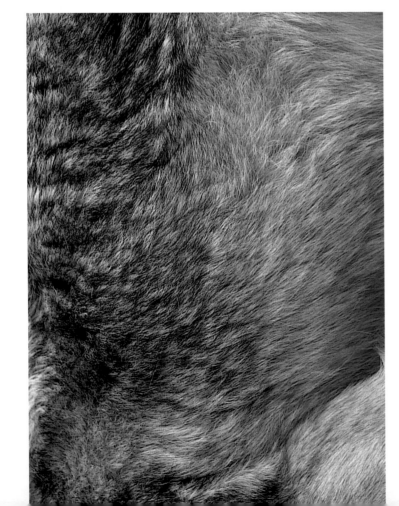

ABOVE: Here, the diversity of colors within a single pelt and some hair growth patterns are apparent. Fur on the wolf's back grows toward its tail, while patterns on the underbelly are more intricate.

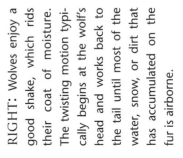

RIGHT: Wolves enjoy a good shake, which rids their coat of moisture. The twisting motion typically begins at the wolf's head and works back to the tail until most of the water, snow, or dirt that has accumulated on the fur is airborne.

Ice does not accumulate on a wolf's coat when the animal exhales its warm, moist breath into its fur, allowing the wolf to keep warm as it curls up and snuggles its nose beneath its bushy tail. In this pose, the wolf can sleep comfortably even when temperatures plunge to forty degrees below zero (-4.5°C).

In the summer months, wolves usually shed their dense underfur to cope with the soaring temperatures. Like dogs and other canids, wolves pant to cool their bodies, breathing in through their noses and out through their mouths. They have sweat glands only between their toes, so the moisture that evaporates through panting is their chief method of regulating their body temperature.

BELOW: This molting wolf is losing its heavy winter coat in time for the warm weather. Late in the summer, it will begin to regrow the thicker, warmer hairs that protect it all winter long.

Wolves are best suited for cold weather, however. Their stocky bodies conserve heat, and their layers of insulating fur keep them warm. Long legs and relatively large feet are ideal for traveling through snow and over ice, and wolves often look to frozen rivers and streams for paths, as they find moving over the ice fairly easy.

While traveling through deep snow, wolves move in single file. The lead wolf blazes the trail, while the others follow behind him through the path he has made. When the lead wolf tires, another takes over, thus conserving the energy of the pack as a whole. Wolves will also make use of paths made by other animals, such as caribou or moose.

RIGHT: The wolf's long legs and narrow chest aid it in running through snow, which covers much of this species' range for large parts of the year. But such movement is extremely tiring and when hunting in snow, wolves will rest as needed after an unsuccessful chase before taking up the hunt again.

LEFT: In their winter travels, the pack usually moves single file to allow those animals behind the leader to conserve energy. Wolves often use the same travel routes over an entire winter, and even over the course of many years. A pack familiar with its territory learns the safest and most efficient paths, following them from year to year. Over the same season, the snow on an oft-traversed course becomes packed, and thus is easier to navigate.

OVERLEAF: A wolf pack jumps a creek. When temperatures are low enough that waterways freeze solid, wolves often prefer to travel over the snow-covered ice. Wind sweeping across the open areas along rivers and over lakes keeps the snow at manageable levels, making travel easier.

A Predator's Most Important Tools

Canids have forty-two teeth, and the wolf is no exception—it has twenty teeth in the upper jaw and twenty-two in the lower. The four all-important canine teeth, which take their name from this revered genus, are long and gently curved, and measure from two to two and a half inches (5–6.4cm) from their roots to their tips. The canine teeth function like vise grips, allowing the wolf to effectively seize and hold its struggling prey.

Wolves also have several other types of teeth, which perform various functions. Carnassial teeth—upper premolars and lower molars—are vital for slicing through meat, muscle, skin, and tendons. Incisors—of which the wolf has twelve, six in the upper jaw and six in the lower—tear the meat from the bone. Molars chew meat and crush bones.

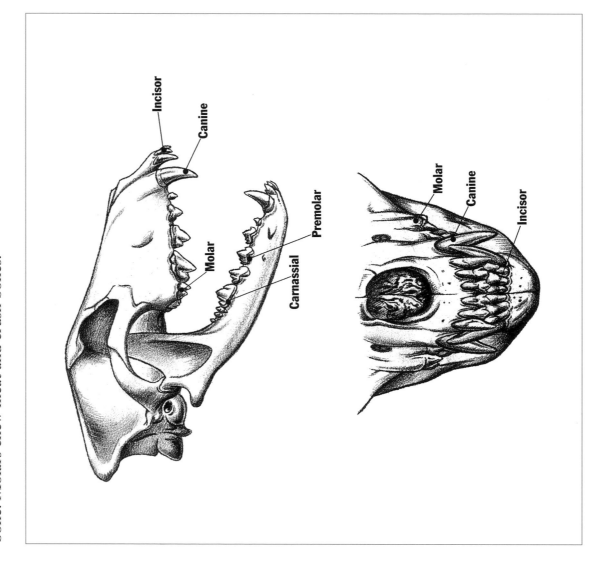

RIGHT: Wolves have a total of forty-two teeth, with twenty in the upper jaw: six incisors, two canines, eight premolars, and four molars. In the lower jaw are twenty-two teeth: six incisors, two canine teeth, eight premolars, and six molars. "Carnassial" refers to larger specialized premolars and molars that are adapted for cutting.

Large, strong teeth and powerful jaw muscles render the bite pressure of a wolf equal to 1,500 pounds per square inch (3,300kg/6.5cm) (compared with 300 pounds per square inch for a human [660kg/6.5cm]). Wolves use this mighty jaw pressure to crack the leg bones of their prey, so they can get to the nutritious marrow.

Wolves depend on their speed and endurance when hunting, so running is, quite literally, essential to their survival—their long legs and sturdy paws are thus well developed for pursuit. Even when they are not hunting,

LEFT: A wolf's jaws and teeth are well-equipped for the grasping, tearing, cutting, and crushing they must do in order to catch, kill, and eat prey with thick hides, tough flesh, and massive bones.

OVERLEAF: Wolves spend much of their time traveling, and can trot for an extended period of time at about eight to ten miles per hour (12.8–16km/h). From spring through fall, when wolves breed and care for young pups, the pack may be on the move but stays relatively close to the den or rendezvous site. In the winter, when the pups are old enough to run with the pack, the wolves range much farther afield.

RIGHT, TOP: A paw print left in soft sand displays the foot structure of the wolf. Back feet have four toes, while front feet have four toes that touch the ground plus a fifth toe placed higher on the leg, called a dew claw.

wolves spend much of their time moving, and are on their feet for as much as a third of their lives. Front feet are larger than hind feet, and leave impressive tracks that can measure more than five inches (12.7cm) across. Each back paw has four toes, while front paws have four toes plus a residual fifth toe called a dew claw. Wolves' claws, which are not retractable like feline claws, provide traction as they run or jump. As wolves walk, their hind feet step into the prints left by their front feet, which makes it easier for the animal to travel through the snow. The paws also spread as the wolf sets its feet down, giving it additional traction on wet or snowy terrain.

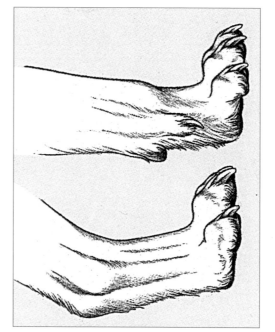

RIGHT, BOTTOM: The dew claw is visible in this illustration of a wolf's hind and front feet. A wolf's foreleg and hind leg on the same side move along the same line, so that it steps with its back foot into the track left by its front foot.

Like dogs, cats, and other animals that must move quickly and quietly, wolves walk and run using digitigrade movement, which means that they move on their toes, with the back part of the foot raised off the ground. Humans, apes, and bears, by contrast, are among the animals that walk and run using plantigrade movement, that is, in a flat-footed fashion.

Digitigrade movement means that wolves can run comfortably at a steady pace for long distances and can maneuver easily, even at great speed. These advantages are critical for an animal that spends so much time on the move—wolves typically walk, lope, or run for as many as eight to ten hours a day. A wolf's most common gait is a trot, which it can maintain at a pace of approximately five miles per hour (8kph) for long distances. While in pursuit of prey, a wolf can run at speeds averaging twenty-five miles per hour (40.2kph) for a several miles, and can even sprint at about forty miles per hour (64.4kph) for a short duration.

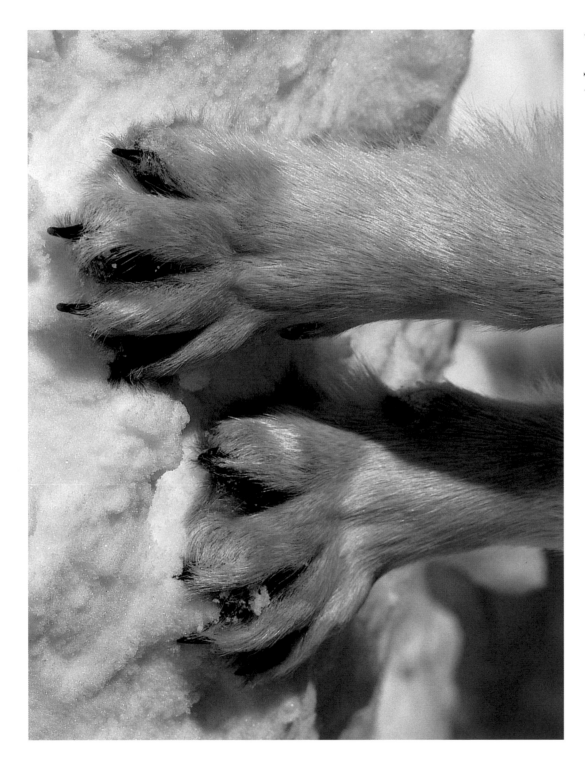

BELOW: Wolf paws have tough pads on the bottom and each toe has a blunt claw, which helps the wolf gain traction on difficult terrain. Between the toe and heel pads are coarse hairs that provide additional traction and also keep the animal's feet warm.

Relying on Their Senses

Their keen sense of smell is perhaps more important to wolves than any other sense in successfully tracking their prey; they also use their sense of smell to recognize the boundaries established by other wolf packs. By sniffing a trail or a marked area, wolves can assess what type of animal left the scent, the number of animals who passed that way, how recently they were in the vicinity, and even whether any of the animals were sick or wounded. Given the right wind conditions, wolves can scent their prey up to one and a half miles (2.4km) away.

RIGHT: A wolf's sense of smell is estimated to be one hundred times more sensitive than that of a human. Wolves use their noses to recognize each other through scent, to identify the presence of intruder wolves in their territory, to locate prey, and even to assess the health of the other animals they encounter. Scent marking and patrolling its territory are critical activities for a wolf pack, and wolves have been observed spending twice as much time marking the borders of their territory as they do the interior region.

Jacobsen's organs, small openings in the roof of a wolf's mouth, allow a wolf to "taste" the air, thus improving the sense of smell. When a wolf pauses and sniffs at the air with muzzle raised and lips curled back, it is retrieving sensory information that humans can only begin to imagine.

A wolf's hearing, too, is incredibly acute. It can hear the howls of other wolves at least six miles (9.6km) away, and possibly much farther. Like dogs, wolves can detect high-pitched frequencies that are inaudible to the human ear.

While hearing and a superb sense of smell are perhaps most critical to a wolf, its vision is sharp as well, at least in its ability to detect movement at a great distance. Wolves also have good peripheral vision and night vision, though they are limited in the colors they perceive.

ABOVE: Hearing is the wolf's second most acute sense, after its sense of smell. Some researchers believe that wolves can hear as far as six miles (9.6km) away in woodland and ten miles (16km) in open grassland.

LEFT: Wolves possess excellent night vision and a superior ability to detect movement, which is important when scanning the landscape for prey.

A Precarious Existence

A wolf's life is a dangerous one, and in the wild an individual seldom lives beyond ten years of age—many die much younger. Starvation, disease, and injury are among the leading causes of death for a wild wolf. Wolves may be critically injured by their prey while hunting or in a confrontation with other wolves; they are also commonly injured or killed by humans. Illegal hunting and sanctioned wolf control programs are both responsible for the deaths of some wolves, particularly in areas where there is concern about undesirable contact with humans or predation on livestock. Other wolves are killed by cars or trucks as they cross a road—this is especially likely if a road runs through a pack's territory.

Wolves in captive settings lead safer lives, protected as they are from the dangers of the wild. In captivity, a wolf may live to be thirteen or fourteen years of age.

BELOW: A lone wolf leads an even more uncertain life than wolves protected by a pack. On its own, a wolf may be attacked by wolf packs whose territory it is invading, and it is a far less efficient hunter, relying on small mammals for sustenance rather than on the large ungulates that are wolves' chief prey.

ABOVE: Two wolves engage in a struggle for dominance. While a strong pack hierarchy helps resolve conflicts within a pack, and fights to the death are relatively rare, wolves still do sometimes kill each other in battles for dominance. Wolves may also kill members of rival packs in territorial disputes.

The Red Wolf

True to the animal's common name, the red wolf's coat is indeed reddish, though the fur shows considerable variation within that color range, from deep copper to a shade that can be described as strawberry blonde. The underbelly is often lighter, sometimes creamy, and the animal's face and back may be marked with darker gray-brown or black highlights.

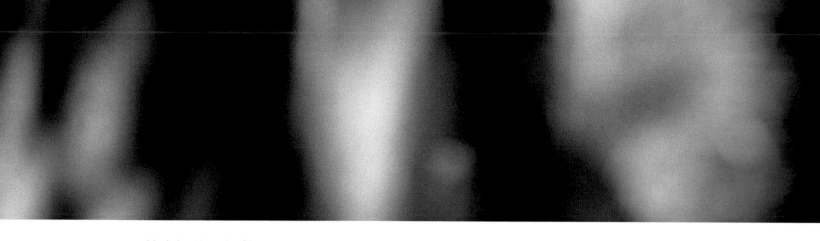

The red wolf (*Canis rufus*) is regarded by some scientists as either a subspecies of the gray wolf or perhaps a hybrid created by the interbreeding of gray wolves and coyotes. But efforts to delist *Canis rufus* as a species have failed, and it is currently classified as distinct from the gray wolf.

Smaller than the gray wolf but larger than the coyote, the red wolf typically stands twenty-eight inches (71.1cm) tall at the shoulder and weighs between forty and eighty pounds (18.1–36.3kg). It measures, on average, fifty-five inches (139.7cm) from nose tip to tail tip, and its body is somewhat rangier than that of the gray wolf. The red wolf is described as more agile than its cousin, and has even been known to jump onto low tree branches.

The red wolf once roamed much of the Southeast, from Florida and Georgia west to Texas and along the Mississippi River from the Gulf of Mexico into Missouri and Illinois, though it is now limited to sites in North Carolina and Tennessee, where populations have recently been reintroduced into the wild.

Not much is known about wild red wolf behavior and habits in the years before recovery efforts, as scientists took little notice of this species until the 1960s, when it was already on the verge of extinction in the wild. Red wolf behavior observed today may be influenced by environmental pressures and by the species' undoubted history of interbreeding with coyotes.

Like gray wolves, red wolves live in packs, though the packs observed tend to be somewhat smaller than many gray wolf packs. It is not clear whether the red wolf's limited population is a determining factor in smaller pack size, or whether red wolf packs simply tend to be more compact.

Nutrias, deer, rabbits, squirrels, raccoons, and birds are the chief prey of red wolves, who have also been known to prey on domestic pets and livestock, though not in significant numbers. Their home range of the Southeast lacks the large ungulates of the north and the Great Plains, such as moose, elk, and buffalo, and this dependence on smaller prey may explain in part the smaller size of both the animals themselves and of their packs.

OPPOSITE: By the 1960s, the red wolf population had been severely compromised by hunting and trapping and by habitat loss. Unable to find mates among their own species, red wolves began to interbreed with coyotes, leading red wolves to the brink of extinction. Today, conservationists are working to preserve red wolves through captive breeding programs and reintroduction efforts.

A Range Far and Wide

The gray wolf thrived as a hunter in part because of its superior ability to survive and adapt to a great number of different climates and habitats. At one time the most widely distributed land mammal in the world, *Canis lupus* ranged across almost the entirety of the Northern Hemisphere, from the icy Arctic to verdant woodlands to open grasslands.

RIGHT, TOP: At one time, wolves were distributed across most of the Northern Hemisphere, inhabiting nearly every type of environment except for vast deserts and tropical rain forests. Systematic persecution of predators and destruction of their habitat by encroaching humans resulted in a shrinking geographical range and declining wolf numbers.

This extraordinary capacity for survival in a wide range of environments no doubt saved the wolf from extinction. As humans encroached on their preferred territories, wolves were able to retreat to more mountainous or thickly forested lands from the open plains that favored group hunting.

RIGHT, BOTTOM: Historically, Mexican wolves inhabited central Mexico and ranged through western Texas, Arizona, and New Mexico. These shy creatures preferred forested highlands, where cover was dense, and food and water were plentiful. Today, this subspecies is being preserved through captive breeding and reintroduction programs.

Wolves living in mountainous areas or in the icy regions of the far north developed physical characteristics that allowed them to cope with the extreme environments. Thus Arctic wolves have longer, thicker coats and stockier bodies than other North American wolf subspecies. Likewise, wolves that live in hot, dry climates have shorter hair, longer legs, and rangier bodies than those living farther north.

In the past few decades, activists have emphasized the necessity of preserving habitats for wolves and of protecting them from threats by humans, and their efforts have led to reintroductions and recoveries of wolf populations in many areas. Only time will tell whether humans will make space in a permanent way for their wild wolf neighbors.

BELOW: Wolves need protected areas in national parks and wildlife refuges if they are to survive in the wild. Cities, suburbs, farms, and ranches have eaten up much of the wolf's traditional range, forcing this animal into smaller and smaller wilderness areas.

OVERLEAF: Viewing a wolf in a wild setting is a rare treat, and one that often requires a discerning eye.

41

CHAPTER

TWO

LIVING IN
WOLF SOCIETY

A Wolf Pack Is a Family

Wolves live together in relatively complex social groups, which are really wolf families. A pack is usually made up of an adult male and female wolf and their offspring of various ages, but it may also include siblings of one of the alpha pair and, more rarely, unrelated adults who have joined the pack. The social bond between mated pairs and between parent and young, as well as among littermates, is very strong, forged by intense or prolonged physical contact and long association. These bonds, together with a highly developed sense of pack hierarchy, allow wolves to hunt cooperatively, care for pups, and settle their differences with a minimum of danger to individuals and disturbance to the pack as a whole.

Pack sizes vary from two to twenty wolves, with most having between four and seven members. Much larger packs, containing thirty or more wolves, have been reported, though large packs are rather unstable and tend to dissolve quickly into smaller units. In northern regions of North America, primarily in northern Canada and Alaska, packs tend to be larger than is the norm in the lower forty-eight, and include about ten animals. While a pack usually stays together, there are times when a member will splinter off or the pack will break up into smaller groups for short periods of time, typically only a matter of hours or days.

The size of a pack depends on a number of factors, not all of which are well understood, but which include the dimensions of the available territory, the number and size of the available prey, and the stresses on the animals that typically occur in large packs. An area abundant with more substantial prey such as buffalo, moose, or elk, can sustain a larger pack, and indeed, a greater number

PAGES 44–45: Wolves are intensely social animals that form strong attachments to one another, which helps to hold the pack together in a cohesive unit.

OPPOSITE: Wolf packs are typically led by a large, decisive, mature male. He directs the activities of the pack, choosing when to give chase to prey, when to rest, and what travel route to follow, but there is evidence that the leader is influenced by the behavior of his pack mates.

of wolves are required to safely and successfully bring down such massive animals. But packs usually remain smaller than could be efficiently fed; researchers theorize that social stress brought about by too many animals together in one group also plays a critical role in the size of a pack. The competition for food, mates, and dominance effectively prevents very large permanent packs from forming. Pack size is also somewhat fluid, and changes as pups are born and as older offspring leave their natal packs—the packs in which they were born—to find mates and start new packs.

Wolf packs have their own established structure and well-defined rules of conduct, and familiarity with the different ranks of animals and their role in the pack is important in understanding much of wolf behavior. The alpha male and female are the dominant animals in the pack, and typically are the only ones to breed, though occasionally, especially in years when prey is abundant, other wolves in the pack produce pups as well.

Within every pack is a dominance hierarchy that includes the alpha pair; subordinates, including beta wolves; pups; and omega wolves. Each member has a role, and the alpha wolves work hard to maintain the status quo, though they may be challenged by younger wolves hoping to move up in the pack's hierarchy.

PAGES 48–49: Pack mates seem to enjoy each others' company. Most of the members of a pack are extended family, though occasionally an unrelated wolf will successfully join the group.

LEFT: The wolf's expressive face and many variations of body language help it communicate effectively with its pack mates, with unknown wolves, and even with humans and other animals. Good communication between pack members and acceptance of the established dominance hierarchy promote pack stability.

HIERARCHY OF THE PACK

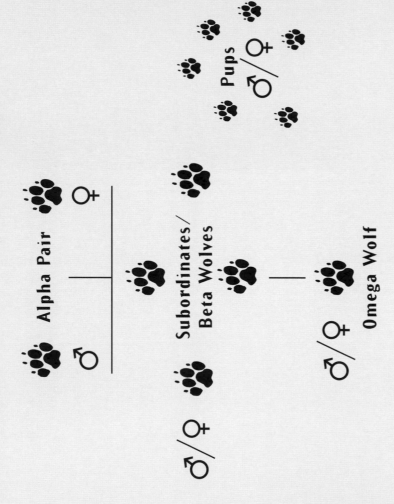

Alpha Pair

♂ ♀

Subordinates/ Beta Wolves

♂/♀

Pups

♂/♀

♂/♀

Omega Wolf

ALPHA PAIR

The dominant adult male and female wolves. These are typically the only wolves to breed, and they often direct the activities of the pack.

BELOW: An alpha pair rests together. Alpha males and females maintain a close bond, which becomes even more intense during the mating season.

SUBORDINATES/BETA WOLVES

Adults and young members of the pack. Males and females may each have their separate dominance hierarchy, though this is not always the case. The second-ranking male and female wolves are called beta wolves. Each wolf's relative position among the subordinates may shift around as they vie with each other for status.

ABOVE: Alpha and beta wolves must constantly assert their dominance over the other members of their pack. Mature subordinate wolves often jockey for position, hoping to move up in relative dominance.

Pups

Pups are somewhat removed from the hierarchy of the overall pack, but they compete with each other for dominance. As with subordinate wolves, the hierarchy among pups changes frequently.

BELOW: Pups do not become part of the overall social hierarchy of the pack until they are two years of age, though they do vie for status with one another.

Omega Wolves

There may be one or more omega wolves living on the edge of the wolf pack. They are tolerated by the pack (that is, they are not driven off), but are often harassed by the other wolves.

ABOVE: Omega wolves rank very low in the social order, and hang about on the periphery of the pack.

ABOVE: Wolves usually behave in fairly predictable social patterns, which maintains the stability of the group. Here, a subordinate wolf (in the middle) shows submission to the alpha male of the pack. Note the bold stance and confident tail position of the dominant wolf.

Alpha wolves are usually the most experienced members of the pack, and often guide the pack's activities. Many researchers observe, however, that other wolves, too, may direct the pack, with the democracy echoing that of a human family: the subordinates are given some decision-making power but the alpha wolves maintain ultimate authority.

It is sometimes said that alpha wolves are made, not born. That is, alpha wolves are not necessarily physically or mentally superior to their fellow wolves, but rather gain their leadership ability through maturity and experience. In fact, many alpha wolves were at one time subordinate wolves in their natal packs. When such a wolf leaves its pack and finds a mate, he or she becomes an alpha wolf in its own new pack.

The social structure of the wolf pack is so significant that the unexpected death of a leader can cause confusion and serious upheaval within the pack, particularly when that death is caused by human intervention, which can be a

54

stressor to the pack in any event. While a certain amount of social competition and restructuring is normal, it takes time for a young wolf to learn the skills necessary to lead the pack. When an alpha wolf in his prime is killed, before a subordinate is ready to move into the role of alpha animal, the pack may become unstable and find itself in danger of disintegrating.

Below the alpha wolves in rank are the mature subordinates. These subordinate wolves usually do not mate and produce young, though there are exceptions, especially in years when prey species are plentiful, and the pack is amply fed. The second-ranking wolves in the pack are known as beta wolves—if any wolves other than the alpha pair do reproduce, it will typically be the beta wolves. There is some jockeying for position among the subordinates, with different wolves moving up and down in rank as they challenge each other for relative dominance. When an alpha male grows old or sick, he may be challenged by one of the subordinates. If the challenge is successful, the alpha male may become the lowest-ranking wolf in the pack or even be driven from the pack entirely.

The lowest-ranking members of the wolf pack are the omega wolves, who often hang about on the periphery of the pack and are worried by the higher-ranking members. These wolves are relegated to eating whatever scraps remain from the kills, after all the other wolves above them in the pack hierarchy have eaten their fill. In lean times, an omega wolf may not have the opportunity to feed at all.

BELOW: A low-ranking wolf displays a submissive pose in reaction to the threats of three more dominant wolves. The threatened wolf lies on the ground, exposing its side and belly, with its ears flattened back close to its head.

Pups are unranked in the scheme of the pack as a whole, but there is a pecking order even among the young. This order is very fluid, with first one pup seeming to play the alpha role, then another supplanting it. In this way, the pups practice dominating the others and begin to learn how to function within the tightly knit society of a wolf pack. Though pups are usually the product of the alpha pair's union, they are well tolerated and cared for by all the members of the pack.

New packs form as wolves reach maturity and leave the pack in which they were born to find mates. These pairs become the alpha wolves of their own packs, which fill out and become established as the wolves bear young. Packs may also form when a pack too large to function well splits into two or more smaller packs.

Some wolves never leave their natal packs, and remain as subordinate wolves, waiting for their opportunity to move up within the pack when an alpha wolf becomes too old or sick to lead. These wolves are known as "biders" because they bide their time until they can rise in the pack's hierarchy.

Wolves are nearly always monogamous within any given period, though a wolf may have more than one mate during his or her lifetime. If a wolf's mate dies or is supplanted and must leave the pack, the remaining wolf may choose a new mate.

LEFT: As this subordinate wolf is approached by a more dominant animal, it tucks its tail between its legs, ducks its head, and crouches low in an effort to look small and unthreatening. Its facial expression will also reflect its submissive attitude, with ears laid back, eyes lowered or averted, and lips pulled back.

ABOVE: A young wolf unwilling to wait to move up in the social hierarchy may leave the pack of its birth. These dispersers live on their own until they are able to find a mate and form a new pack. Some lone wolves are older individuals who have lost their mates and been forced to leave the safety of the pack.

Lone Wolves

Intensely social animals, wolves rarely choose the life of a loner. A wolf on its own—called a "disperser"—is extremely vulnerable. Hunting is more dangerous and on the whole far less successful than with a pack, and neighboring wolf packs tend to be hostile to lone wolves trespassing on their territory.

When a wolf leaves the security of the pack, it is usually out of necessity: the animal has been driven from the pack by higher-ranking members or it is ready to seek a mate of its own, and is not willing to wait until it can move up in its natal pack. By the age of two, a self-assured and capable young wolf may become a disperser, hoping to find a mate and lead its own pack. The winter breeding season and the spring birthing season are the most common times for wolves to leave their packs in search of a mate. Motivated by sexual need or forced out by the arrival of a new litter and its resulting pressures on the pack, these lone animals travel the areas between established wolf territories or move into territories that are not in use.

Wolf Talk

Wolves use a number of different methods to communicate, both with other members of the pack and with neighboring packs. Among these are vocalizations—including howls, barks, growls, and whimpers—body posture, facial expressions, and scent marking.

Good communication is essential to the health of the pack, as subtle signals convey and reinforce the social hierarchy and allow wolves to settle their differences with shows of dominance and conciliation rather than with physical confrontations. A growl or a nip from the alpha wolf and a conciliatory gesture such as a bowed head and a tucked tail from the offending subordinate can defuse tensions and avoid a fight in which one or more animals might be wounded or even killed. Because all the members are integral to the pack's well-being, wolves do everything they can to prevent injury to their packmates.

BELOW: With its crouching posture, pulled-back lips, nuzzling gesture, and pawing movements, this subordinate wolf is signaling its acceptance of the dominant wolf's position. When wolves communicate clearly their roles within the pack, serious aggression is unnecessary.

ABOVE: Wolves seem to enjoy a good group howl, which is often accompanied by great excitement and tail-wagging. When the pack howls in a chorus, one wolf usually begins and is joined at intervals by others after its first few howls.

From Howls to Whimpers

Perhaps the most widely recognized signature of the wolf is its haunting howl. Each wolf has its own unique voice and howls on a different note; when even a pack of three howls together, the wolves create the impression of a much larger group. Wolves in a pack recognize the voices of other pack members, and sometimes howl to reinforce their identity as a group.

Wolves howl for a number of reasons: to reunite the pack before or after a hunt or when they have become separated while traveling; to alert other packs that they are in the area; and when they sense an intruder in their territory. They also may howl upon awakening or when looking for a mate. Perhaps most interestingly, wolves sometimes howl when none of these reasons seems to hold true; researchers suspect that they do it for the sheer joy it brings them.

While many people believe that wolves howl at the moon, this is not true. They howl more frequently in the evening and in the early morning because that is when they are most active, but they also howl during the daytime. Wolves lift their muzzles into the air to project their powerful voices over the maximum distance, not to direct their howl at the moon.

In addition to howls, a wolf's vocabulary includes whines, whimpers, squeaks, squeals, snarls, growls, and barks. Snarling and growling convey aggression or a threat to another wolf, while whimpering and whining are generally submissive noises. High-pitched whining can also be a sound of greeting, or may accompany a playful romp or pups' requests for food. Barking is relatively unusual among wolves, and is almost always a signal of alarm. Captive wolves living in proximity to domestic dogs have been observed to bark more frequently, presumably having picked up the habit from their fellow canines.

BELOW: While all the reasons for howling are not known, one of the chief functions appears to be assembling the pack. It has also been observed that wolves howl with greater frequency near the borders of their territory, perhaps advertising their claim, and adjacent packs will sometimes reply to the howls of a nearby wolf pack.

Picking up Visual Cues

Wolves' understanding of where they belong in the social order of the pack is expressed in their posture and in their gestures toward their packmates. A subordinate may approach an alpha wolf with its body slung low to the ground and its ears laid flat back against its head; it reaches up to lick the alpha wolf's muzzle or nuzzle its face in a sign of greeting. This behavior, in which wolves explicitly convey their subordinate position, is known as active submission.

As important as it is that subordinate wolves show submission to alpha animals, it is just as crucial to pack stability that dominant wolves act out their leadership roles unequivocally. They do this by looking their subordinates in the eye and by communicating through their posture that they are in charge. Alpha animals bear themselves with confidence, with their tails in an upright position or held straight out behind them.

When wolves interact, the way they hold their ears and tails provides a clue to their position in the pack. Subordinate wolves generally keep their tails hanging down, in a sign of submissiveness, and the lowest-ranking wolves tuck their tails between their legs. A low-ranking wolf will flatten its ears against its head when approaching the alpha wolf. Dominant wolves, by contrast, stand tall and hold their tails high and their ears erect.

Mood, too, can influence the way a wolf carries its ears and tail. A relaxed wolf will hold its tail down in a neutral position, while a fearful wolf will cower with its tail tucked between its legs and its ears laid back, in a sight all too familiar to dog owners who have just scolded their pets. Wolves feeling self-assured hold their tails upright and their ears high. Tail-wagging is common when wolves are happy and want to play.

ABOVE: This wolf conveys its submissive status through body language; in a stance of active submission, it approaches a group of more dominant wolves (out of view) in a low crouch, with ears flat and tail tucked to advertise its acceptance of the hierarchy.

LEFT, TOP: Relaxed but alert, this adult wolf holds its ears high and its tail in a downward position that expresses its contented demeanor. This stance is common in wolves that are observing the landscape but not expecting a threat.

LEFT, BOTTOM: A wolf confident of its high social position holds its tail high and its ears in an alert mode. The animal's pleasant facial expression and gently curving open mouth convey the impression that the wolf is smiling.

If a wolf intends to convey aggression, it will point its ears forward and stand tall, with all its hairs bristling and its teeth bared; its hackles, the erectile hairs on its neck and back, are particularly eloquent. A full-grown wolf in this commanding stance is sufficiently intimidating that the target of its threat—whether another wolf, a human, or another animal—usually thinks seriously about retreating.

Facial expressions also play a part in a wolf's ability to communicate. A knitted brow and bared teeth send a message of aggression, while a playful expression with lips pulled back resembles a wolf "smile." Markings on the face accentuate the wolf's features and underscore its expressions: its eyes are outlined in black and typically surrounded by lighter-colored fur. The muzzle is usually white, which highlights the animal's black lips and nose, and dark fur accents the edges of the ears. When a wolf combines facial expressions with body posture and vocalizations, it leaves little doubt as to the message it is conveying.

RIGHT: Teeth bared and brow furrowed, this wolf prepares to aggressively defend its portion at a deer kill. If this animal were threatening another, less dominant wolf, its facial expression would be much the same, but its ears would be erect and pointed forward.

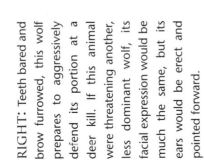

OPPOSITE: Markings on a wolf's face serve to emphasize its expressions. Dark fur along the outer ear, paired with lighter fur inside, make ear positions more noticeable, while black outlines around the wolf's eyes, together with lighter fur surrounding the eye or paler "eyebrows," accentuate the gaze. Light fur along the muzzle draws attention to the wolf's black lips.

RIGHT: Wolves have glands between the pads of their toes that leave a scent when the animal scratches. It is thought that scratching on trees also presents a visual clue to intruding wolves that a pack is already living within a particular territory.

Marking the Spot

Wolves' keen sense of smell lets them pick up cues left by other wolves, and they are adept at recognizing the scents left by their own packmates versus those left by wolves from rival packs. Scent glands between a wolf's toes distribute its scent as it travels, but a wolf also marks its territory with urine. Wolves patrol their territories, marking as they go. Borders with another pack's territory are marked especially vigorously, though some packs maintain buffer zones between their separate territories. Alpha wolves have been observed to leave a scent mark or examine a mark approximately every two minutes when they are busy inspecting their borders.

Establishing and defending a territory are important business for a wolf pack—their very survival depends on it. Because wolves hunt and raise their young within the boundaries of their territory, their access to food and their ability to protect their pups depend on clearly marking and defending their chosen territory. If a pack allowed other wolves to encroach on its territory, prey might be depleted to the point that the land couldn't support the pack.

Territories range in size from fifty square miles (30sq km) to thousands of square miles, depending on a number of factors. The size of the pack, the terrain, the availability of prey, and whether the chief prey is migratory all play a role in how many wolves a specific area can support.

LEFT: Subordinate female wolves squat (males stand on all fours) to urinate; this is a less effective method of scent marking because the scent is distributed lower to the ground, but the mark is left behind nevertheless.

OPPOSITE, BOTTOM: When scent marking with urine, alpha wolves, including alpha females, raise their legs. Wolves typically scent mark more frequently along the borders of their territory, but they also mark within it, most likely leaving scent messages that advertise their dominance to the pack.

The Politics of the Pack

Like subordinates of every description all over the world, lower-ranking wolves sometimes try to contest the authority of the dominant wolf, and in this case the alpha wolf must assert control. A steady stare may be all that is needed to subdue the misbehaving wolf, or the alpha wolf may have to adopt a threat pose, growling with teeth bared and hackles raised. Grasping the subordinate wolf's muzzle with its own mouth is another tactic the alpha wolf may use to declare its dominance, or it may put its paws on the challenging animal's shoulders to proclaim its own power.

ABOVE: A steady stare or a quick snarl may be all an alpha wolf needs to bring a subordinate back in line. Low-ranking wolves will immediately seek to appease the dominant wolf, though animals closer in rank to the alpha may stare back in challenge.

RIGHT: Dominance postures include what famed wolf biologist David L. Mech has termed "riding up." In an unmistakable display of authority, the dominant wolf stands with its front legs on the back or shoulders of a lower-ranking wolf, asserting its power not only to the wolf involved but to the rest of the pack as well.

In a lupine form of crying uncle, a wolf that is ready to accept its subordinance will turn onto its side or back and expose its stomach to the dominant animal in a show of vulnerability. This passive submission conveys the subordinate wolf's acceptance of the status quo and acknowledges the superior position of the dominant animal.

These ritualized declarations and confirmations of status contribute to pack stability. They allow wolves to avoid serious fights, although animals vying for a vacant alpha position may resort to a physical battle. In part because most wolf packs are made up of mates and related animals with strong bonds, members of the pack are invested in maintaining peace.

ABOVE: Rolling onto its back is an act of passive submission. With this behavior, the subordinate wolf acknowledges its inferiority to the approaching animal. When each wolf understands its position in the social order and behaves accordingly, the pack remains harmonious.

While serious fighting may be rare, smaller skirmishes do break out. Alpha females become more aggressive toward other females during the mating season. Wolves also regularly abuse an omega wolf, attacking it if it hovers too close to the edge of the pack, though they rarely injure the omega wolf seriously. There may also be tussles over a kill, with wolves snarling at each other and tugging at the same pieces of carcass.

BELOW: Wolves are oriented toward each other's mouths, and an alpha animal may gently grasp another wolf's muzzle in its teeth. Subordinates also sometimes hold the leader's muzzle when greeting him.

Wolves at Play

Wolf pups are extremely playful, and adults will take time out for play as well, though far less frequently than juveniles. When wolves play, a certain amount of role reversal is permissible: a dominant wolf may play the submissive, while a low-ranking wolf will "pretend" to be the dominant one. All the wolves appear to understand that these roles are temporary and that the behavior is purely part of having fun.

Wolves have their own language of play—they growl or bark excitedly, and may nip each other as well. When a wolf crouches with its paws out in front of it with its wagging tail high in the air, it is inviting its packmate to play. If the wolf who has been approached is game, it will move closer, at which point the first wolf will either turn and dash away or pounce mischievously. The two will then mock fight or engage in chase games until they run out of energy.

ABOVE: Chase games are a favorite of wolves; when one wolf "catches" the other, the two will mock fight. When adults play together, they often relax the rules of the social hierarchy.

71

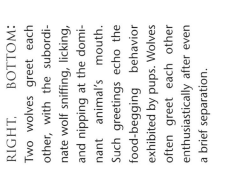

RIGHT, TOP: Tug-of-war is most common among adult wolves when they are competing for meat at a kill, though it is a game pups play often with sticks, bits of animal hide, or bones. Here, two adult wolves tug on a stick.

RIGHT, BOTTOM: Two wolves greet each other, with the subordinate wolf sniffing, licking, and nipping at the dominant animal's mouth. Such greetings echo the food-begging behavior exhibited by pups. Wolves often greet each other enthusiastically after even a brief separation.

ABOVE: Mock fighting is part of wolves' play behavior. They wrestle and gently bite each other, and will sometimes then dash off to initiate a game of chase. As they play together, wolves often bark in loud excitement, a sound they otherwise rarely make except in alarm.

HUNTING:
A GROUP
EFFORT

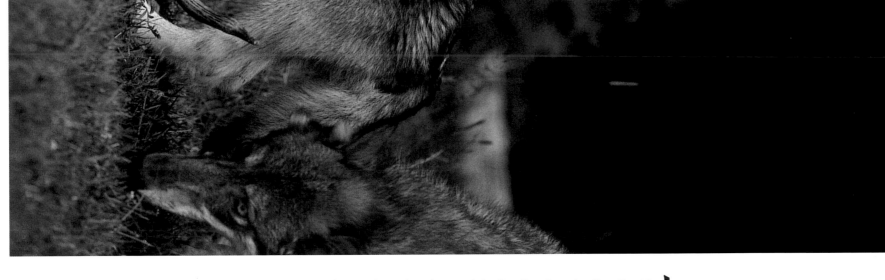

Hunting: A Group Effort

Like many other successful predators, wolves have been maligned at times for what is perceived as their savagery or viciousness during the kill, but in fact they are simply fulfilling a basic need: to feed themselves and their young. Because wolves are carnivores, they must kill other animals in order to eat; they cannot elect to become vegetarians or even balanced omnivores. The species *Canis lupus* evolved over hundreds of thousands of years to occupy a specific ecological niche, and this specialization demands that it hunt and eat the large hoofed mammals that range through its territory.

And while hunting clearly sustains the wolves, it is ultimately good for prey species and the environment as well. By preying on sick or weak animals, wolves actually help strengthen herds of ungulates by eliminating animals that may be genetically inferior. Wolves also target young animals, reducing the number of ungulates overall and thus helping to prevent dangerous overpopulation of deer, moose, elk, caribou, bison, and other such species. When the populations of large mammals such as these go unchecked, the result can be serious damage to the environment due to overbrowsing of vegetation, as well as starvation of the animals when food becomes scarce.

Wolves, like sharks, are at the top of their food chain; they are what is known as apex predators. All the animals in the chain have their part to play, and while it is easy to feel sympathy for those being eaten and perhaps even to blame those doing the killing, it is simply the pattern of nature that has evolved over millions of years and is a requirement of a healthy ecosystem.

PAGES 74–75: Wolves may travel as many as thirty-two miles (51.4km) a day in search of prey. They often travel single file, and when they scent their prey, the pack stops and faces the same direction, sniffing the wind with ears alert, ready to give chase.

LEFT: Young wolves gnaw at the head of an elk. When the wolf pups are old enough, pack members will sometimes lead the pups back to a kill rather than bringing the food to the den or rendezvous site.

A Team Approach

Cooperative hunting is the chief reason that wolves have risen so successfully to the top of their food chain. As wolves were evolving, large mammals represented an excellent food source, and there was relatively little competition for this prey, as few predators could bring down a full-sized moose, elk, bison, or other ungulate. This open ecological niche of top predator offered an opportunity for *Canis lupus*, but a single wolf could not hope to succeed regularly against a herd of ungulates. A pack of wolves working together, however, could achieve what a lone wolf could not.

Wolves typically hunt at night, or in the early morning or evening hours, assembling with a group howl to prepare for the hunt. A pack designates a meeting place, known as a rendezvous site, where it congregates. Pups, guarded by a subordinate wolf, wait at this site while the adults hunt. For a period of about eight to ten weeks in the spring, when pups are born, the pack will use the den site as the rendezvous site, so the youngsters can stay safe in the den.

Hunting successfully in packs is far from simple, however. All the individuals must be committed to the common cause, and they must be physically strong, intelligent, and capable of accepting their given roles within the structure of the pack. A complex and risky endeavor, hunting cooperatively does not guarantee success even when a pack is large, healthy, and well organized. The success rate, in fact, is estimated at approximately 10 percent—for every ten attempts at a kill, wolves come away with a meal only once.

As fast and clever as wolves may be, their prey are often more than a match for them. Deer and caribou can typically outrun a wolf pack, and a healthy moose will turn and face the pack with dangerous antlers and hooves ready to gore any wolf who ventures too close. Experienced wolves know that a prey animal at a physical disadvantage is a surer proposition, and they carefully select diseased, maimed, weak, old, or very young animals to increase their chances of making the kill. It simply doesn't make sense for the pack to exhaust itself chasing healthy, full-sized animals that are unlikely to be caught.

Because large ungulates can typically outrun wolves, the pack must form a strategy that levels the playing field. One distinct advantage that wolves can often call upon is the element of surprise: they will advance on their prey from downwind, to avoid being scented by the herd, and will move as close as possible before launching an attack. Sometimes wolves will split up and circle around the herd; by the time the animals detect the wolves' presence, they are surrounded by the pack.

OPPOSITE: Predators are experts at scenting and sighting the most vulnerable of their potential prey. They zero in on the young, the old, and the weak or sick in order to have the best chance at making the kill. If a pack can separate a weak individual from the rest of the herd, the kill becomes largely a matter of time.

Before a pack decides to pursue an animal, it surreptitiously evaluates the situation, moving quietly and efficiently so as to avoid detection. If the herd should see or scent the pack, it may have the chance to escape before the wolves can move into place for an attack. Even if the wolves are able to prevent the animals from fleeing, a herd that has ample warning can position itself defensively, with young and weak animals at the center of the herd, and robust, full-grown animals on the outside.

To determine whether the energy they are likely to expend will be worthwhile, wolves commonly "test" their quarry before they commit to full pursuit. They force the animal they have targeted to either run or defend itself, and then they quickly appraise the situation. If their intended prey is

more aggressive in defending itself than they had expected, they consider giving up the chase and moving on. Because all the members are integral to the pack's well-being, wolves carefully assess the risk of injury when confronting truculent prey. A mature male moose or bison can critically wound or kill a wolf, and if the intended quarry appears well prepared to mount a vigorous defense, the risk may not be worth it for the pack.

Wolves are adept at identifying animals in poor health, and they will choose to pursue those animals that appear wounded, lame, or easily winded. The pack will also select calves that can be efficiently separated from their mothers. In addition to the signs of weakness that may be obvious to us, wolves are apparently attuned to a myriad of less visible symptoms that may indicate that a prey animal is not in optimum health. While researchers are not certain what these subtle clues are, they may range from the scent an animal gives off to nearly imperceptible changes in its gait.

When the wolves close in on their intended prey, the animal may run instead of turning to defend itself. In this case, the pack will generally give chase, doing its best to separate its target prey from the rest of the herd, wearying it until it collapses. In winter conditions, wolves have a definite advantage over their prey, whose great weight slows them in deep snow and whose hooves slide on ice. Wolves, by contrast, not only have paws that spread as they step, giving them relatively good traction on snow and ice, but their lighter weight also means that they are often able to run across the snow's icy crust without breaking through like their larger, heavier quarry.

If the pack must pursue an animal over some distance, it will often employ a strategy designed to tire the prey while allowing the wolves to keep pace: as the pack pursues its target, one wolf chases the animal closely, harrying it by biting at its legs and body. When the lead wolf becomes fatigued, another assumes its place. By taking turns at staying close on the heels of its prey, the pack increases its chances of success in eventually tiring the swifter ungulate. Once the prey animal becomes exhausted, the wolves are all but assured of a meal.

Wolves will cut the chase short abruptly if they sense that their selected prey is fleeter of foot than they anticipated. The pack must prudently balance its investment of energy with the likelihood of success—if a kill seems doubtful, wolves won't waste valuable time and energy pursuing an animal.

OPPOSITE: A wolf stalks a caribou, biting at its legs to slow its progress. The pack will harry an animal it has chosen to chase, snapping at its side, rump, thighs, and neck until the quarry falters. The wolves then lunge at the animal to drop it to the ground.

A SNAPSHOT
OF THE WOLF'S PREY

LEFT: In some regions, the beaver is an important supplement to the wolf diet; a beaver cut off from water is a fairly easy catch.

BEAVER

Wolves will generally elect to hunt larger prey, but beavers play an important role in the wolf's diet when other prey is not available.

BISON

The largest prey that wolves face, male bison weigh as much as 800 to 2,000 pounds (363.2–908kg); cows weigh 400 to 1.000 pounds (181.6–454kg). When attacked by wolves, bison will often turn in a mass and face the pack with low-ered horns. They will also strike at wolves with their hooves.

ABOVE: Bison, historically a main prey animal of wolves in the West, are among the most dangerous of the wolf's quarry. As with many of the wolf's prey, calves are particularly vulnerable.

CARIBOU

Caribou are common prey for wolves living in the far north. These animals are fleeter of foot than wolves, and their massive herd size and migrations can make them challenging prey.

DALL SHEEP

Dall sheep are among the prey species of wolves living in Alaska. When wolves attack, these sure-footed sheep flee up craggy precipices where wolves find it difficult to follow.

DEER

While deer may seem like mild animals, they possess sharp hooves that can critically wound or kill a wolf. But turning in defense is a deer's last resort. Deer protect themselves by being attentive to their surroundings and fleeing at the first sign of danger.

OPPOSITE, BOTTOM: Caribou are migratory animals, and there is evidence that some wolf packs follow them on their migrations. Because the caribou become somewhat used to the wolves' presence, only the animals nearest the predators are wary.

ABOVE: Dall sheep often flee up rocky hills, so wolves try to attack from higher ground, cutting off this avenue of escape.

RIGHT: Deer are the smallest ungulates that wolves prey upon, but they are among the fastest. Especially in deep snow, deer have the distinct advantage of speed.

83

Elk

Bulls average 700 pounds (317.8kg), while cows average 500 pounds (227kg), and both have dangerous hooves. Males also have pointed antlers that can easily gore a wolf who ventures too close. Elk will sometimes turn and defend themselves against wolves, but they are faster than moose and will often decide to flee.

Moose

An adult male moose weighs 1.000 to 1.250 pounds (454–567.5kg) and can run at a speed of approximately 35 miles per hour (56.3kpm). Females are slightly smaller, tipping the scales at 800 to 850 pounds (363.2–385.9kg). Because an adult moose is well equipped to defend itself with sharp hoofs—the male is outfitted with dangerous antlers as well—these animals turn and defend themselves more often than they run. The most vulnerable are newborn calves, which are protected by their mothers until they are about a year old.

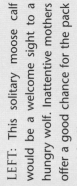

LEFT: This solitary moose calf would be a welcome sight to a hungry wolf. Inattentive mothers offer a good chance for the pack to pick off a youngster.

MOUNTAIN GOAT

When threatened, these goats escape to cliffs and rocky outcroppings, where wolves are at a disadvantage over the exceptionally sure-footed goats.

Musk Ox

The average musk oxen weigh in at more than 700 pounds (317.8kg), and this massive size helps the herd protect itself. The animals will form a circle, facing outward to confront the wolves with large horns and sharp hooves.

OPPOSITE, TOP: Elk, also called wapiti, are a vital prey animal for wolves in western Canada.

RIGHT: Mountain goats can be challenging prey because of their habit of staying close to rocky areas.

BELOW: Musk oxen tend to form a defensive position when attacked by wolves. If the wolves can panic the herd into a stampede, a youngster may get left behind in the confusion.

ABOVE: Wolves have large stomachs, an adaptation to their feast or famine lifestyle. Because they do not have the luxury of feeding whenever they like—and typically make a large kill that they must eat before losing it to another predator or to scavengers— wolves can consume as much as twenty pounds (9kg) of meat at one time. After gorging themselves on such vast amounts of meat, wolves drink a large quantity of water, which aids their digestion.

86

Feast or Famine

When wolves finally bring down their prey, they devour it efficiently, leaving only indigestible parts like hair, hide, and large bones. The hindquarters and internal organs are the most sought-after parts of the animal, and are devoured first, while muscle and sinew are among the least desirable parts of the prey. Wolves even crack open the smaller bones with their powerful jaws and consume the nutrition-rich marrow. Pack members often snarl and squabble over food at a kill as they vie for the choicest pieces of meat, but these conflicts rarely become serious. When food is abundant, fights over food are fairly rare, but wolves at a kill observe the proprieties of the pack hierarchy, and when food is scarce, higher-ranking wolves get better access.

ABOVE: A wolf gnaws on the antler of a fallen moose. Massive molars in the back of the wolf's mouth are designed for crushing bone and antlers. Other teeth help the wolf tear and cut the flesh, fat, and sinew from the bones. Once chunks of meat or other parts are torn from the carcass, much of it is swallowed whole.

87

ABOVE: Gray wolves feed on the carcass of a deer. After a kill, the wolves begin to feed immediately, tearing voraciously at any flesh that has been exposed during the hunt. A small animal, such as a deer, taken down by a large pack may be consumed entirely at one sitting, with only indigestible parts such as large bones, antlers, and bits of hide remaining at the kill site.

BELOW: Typically, the privileges of dominance prevail at a kill, but occasionally, disagreements break out. Such conflicts are most common between animals close in rank, when competition for the choicest meat causes resentments to flare. Alpha animals can claim the favored parts of a kill, with other wolves tearing off pieces according to their relative position in the pack. Once a wolf is in possession of a piece of meat, its ownership is usually not contested.

Because hunting large prey is such a low-percentage affair, wolves are accustomed to a life of feast or famine, and can function efficiently without food for two weeks or more. When they do succeed in a kill, they eat until they cannot eat any more, ultimately consuming as much as twenty pounds of meat per wolf. When the pack is unable to finish the entire kill, the wolves may cache any leftovers—usually burying it in the ground—and return to it later. Quite often, the wolves find upon returning that the cache has been raided by another animal, such as a weasel, a coyote, or a fox. Any parts of the carcass not eaten or cached by the wolves will be eagerly devoured by scavengers such as ravens, foxes, coyotes, and even eagles.

The wolf's digestive system is well equipped to handle meat in massive quantities. A large pancreas and liver help cope with these periodic gluts of meat. Water is also essential to a wolf's diet. Without an adequate supply of water, they can suffer uremic poisoning, a dangerous buildup of toxins in the blood caused by eating large amounts of meat.

After a successful hunt and the enormous meal that follows it, wolves are fully satiated and ready for a well-earned nap, which typically lasts several hours. They'll loll in the sun on warm days, or snuggle up with their tails wrapped around themselves when the weather is brisk.

RIGHT: After gorging themselves, the pack curls up to sleep for several hours. A successful hunt and the feeding frenzy that follows are exhausting, and the wolves rest to recover and to aid digestion of the massive quantity of meat they've just eaten.

FACING OTHER PREDATORS

Wolves and other predators may try to avoid crossing each other's paths, but sometimes confrontation is inevitable.

ALLIGATORS

In the southeastern United States, in the range of the red wolf, alligators pose a threat. These aggressive reptiles have been known to catch and kill red wolves.

BEARS

Bears and wolves have been known to engage in deadly conflict, and they are especially aggressive toward each other when young are involved. Wolves will attack a grizzly or black bear that gets too close to a den site, as bears will sometimes unearth the wolf pups from the den, and kill and eat them. Wolves will also kill bear cubs, and may even prey upon a larger bear that is hibernating and thus vulnerable. A bear sometimes confronts a wolf pack over a kill, and tries to take the carcass for itself, with the wolves defending their prize.

COUGARS

Cougars of both sexes are solitary except during mating season and when females are caring for a litter, and thus are vulnerable to wolf packs that try to seize a kill. A cougar may try to defend its kill, however, and can do serious injury to a wolf with its claws and teeth. Wolves have been known to kill cougar cubs, and may even kill a full-grown cougar, though this is rare.

ABOVE: Alligators may take a red wolf that dares too close to the water.

LEFT: A wolf and a cougar battle over a kill. Because numbers of both wolves and cougars are currently relatively low, encounters between the animals are rare.

COYOTES

Wolves do not care to share their territories with coyotes, and will drive off, and sometimes attack and kill, any coyotes that stray into their territory. Coyotes typically avoid wolves, if possible, establishing ranges between the outer boundaries of wolf pack territories. But coyotes may also take advantage of nearby wolf packs, scavenging leftovers from wolf kills and digging up caches of food the wolves have buried.

Both wolves and coyotes are species in the genus *Canis*, and they are capable of interbreeding. There is some evidence that wolves and coyotes in the southeastern United States have interbred over time. It seems likely that these two species interbreed only when populations of wolves are so low that finding a mate of its own species is untenable for a wolf.

FOXES

Because foxes and wolves do not prey upon the same animals, wolves do not go out of their way to chase foxes out of their territory, though they will attack a fox that is feeding on a kill. When food is scarce, wolves sometimes prey on red foxes; likewise, Arctic foxes become prey for Arctic wolves when times are hard.

WOLVERINES

These small carnivores may be tenacious, but wolves have a decided size advantage, and wolverines are often driven away from a kill by wolves. Sometimes the wolverine will defend its kill, often getting killed in the attempt.

ABOVE: Wolves will not tolerate coyotes in their territories, running off or attacking these close cousins when confronted with them.

RIGHT, TOP: Foxes pose little threat to wolves in terms of competition for prey, and sometimes prove handy, as wolves will expand abandoned fox dens to use as their own.

RIGHT, BOTTOM: Feisty members of the weasel family, wolverines at a kill are sometimes attacked by wolves.

RIGHT: A grizzly bear chases a wolf down a slope. Confrontations between bears and wolves occur mainly when a bear tries to seize a wolf kill or when bears get too close to a pack's den site.

OPPOSITE, TOP: Reinforcements arrive: a second pack member forces the bear to divide its attention. It's possible that the bear is heading in the direction of the wolf den, or perhaps the second wolf simply entered the fray in defense of its packmate.

OPPOSITE, BOTTOM: A grizzly attempts to appropriate a moose carcass, while the somewhat wary wolves try to defend their kill. The wolves may not give up without a fight, but they are rarely able to drive away a determined full-grown bear.

RIGHT, TOP: Small animals play a relatively minor role in the wolf's diet, but they are important sources of food when large prey becomes scarce. This gray wolf has snagged a snowshoe hare.

RIGHT, BOTTOM: Beavers are the smallest animals that make up a main part of the wolf's diet. This wolf has managed to catch a beaver in the water, a difficult feat because beavers are such fast swimmers.

A Diet Varied by Necessity

When large prey is unavailable, wolves will turn to smaller animals, such as beavers, voles, rabbits, muskrats, raccoons, woodchucks, mice, birds, and even shellfish. Wolves hunting alone are likelier to pursue these more manageable types of prey, but a diet consisting of these small animals can't efficiently sustain a large pack. When food becomes scarce, pack size is affected, and wolves may travel in packs of as few as three. Conversely, when larger animals are plentiful pack sizes may grow; it takes about six wolves to efficiently hunt deer and eight or more to challenge aggressive prey such as moose or bison.

While wolves are not generally thought of as scavengers, they will feed on the carrion of animals they did not kill themselves if the opportunity presents itself. When they have gone for a very long time without food, and no opportunity to hunt seems forthcoming, wolves resort to foods like insects, berries, or nuts, though these are not a significant source of nutrition for them.

ABOVE: Wolves have been known to spend hours trying to catch fish, though it is not a mainstay of their diet. A hungry wolf will also feed on mice, snakes, squirrels, birds, grasshoppers, and even berries when times are tough.

RIGHT: When humans replace the wolf's wild prey with domestic animals, these predators often have little choice but to accept the change and begin preying on livestock. Wolves with access to good hunting grounds and wild ungulates nearly always prefer their wild prey.

Wolves typically avoid contact with humans, but if their usual prey is unavailable because of environmental pressures, wolves will also scavenge through garbage cans and dumpsters, and occasionally kill livestock. Opportunity is a key factor in whether wolves kill domestic animals—when their natural prey becomes scarce because humans have replaced woodland with farmland or ranches, wolves will replace wild ungulates with accessible cows and sheep. It is this behavior that earned the wolf a place on bounty hunters' lists, and resulted in its nearly being eradicated in the eighteenth and nineteenth centuries. When wolves kill livestock, they sometimes begin to eat more selectively, leaving parts of the kill behind rather than consuming the entire animal. This behavior has also been noted in other predators, such as mountain lions and foxes, that begin to prey on domestic animals.

With their superior intelligence, strong social bonds, and physical prowess, wolves are well equipped to survive and thrive in the varied terrains in which they live. It is chiefly when humans interfere that wolf packs are threatened, driven by a shrinking habitat and scarcity of prey to kill valuable livestock and thus become hunted themselves.

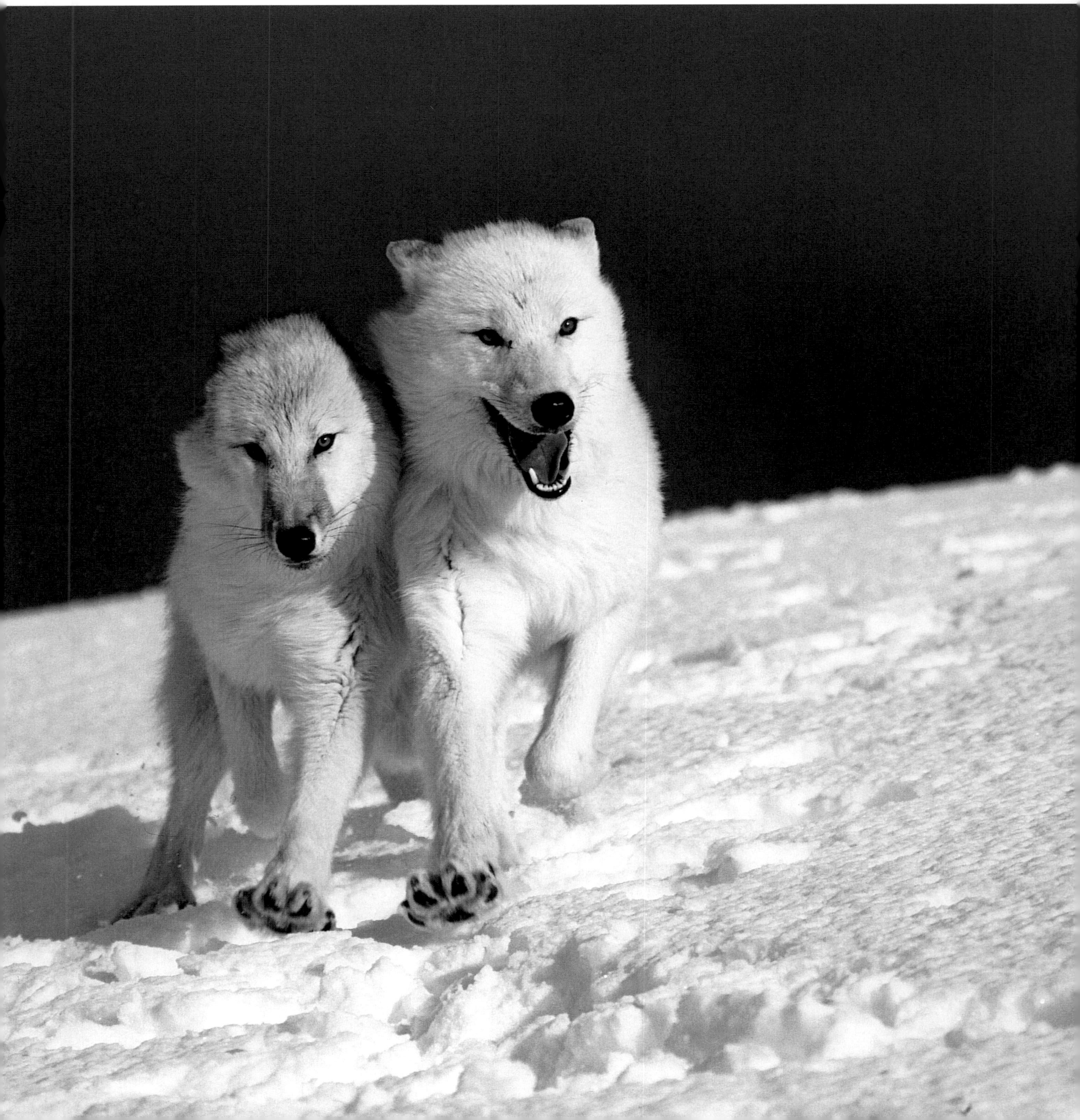

The Next Generation

*P*erhaps one of the most important endeavors a wolf pack undertakes is the production of more wolves, for without healthy young who are well prepared for the rigors of life in the wild, the species cannot survive. The pack approaches this awesome responsibility with the same dedication to teamwork that it displays in living and hunting together, and the new litter is greeted with great enthusiasm by all the wolves.

The Mating Game

Wolves usually have only one mate at a time, though a wolf may have more than one mate over the course of its lifetime. While a pair usually remains faithful to each other, refusing other wolves who approach them to mate, a wolf will select another partner if his or her own mate dies or is expelled from the pack. In most packs, only the alpha male and female breed, though when prey is especially abundant, a second pair may also mate and bear offspring. Occasionally, an alpha male shows little interest in mating, and in this situation the beta wolf moves in and takes over the breeding responsibilities.

Unlike domestic dogs, which can breed twice each year, wolves breed only once in the span of a year. The breeding season is late winter, usually between the end of January and April, depending upon the latitude where the wolves are living. In the far north, where spring comes later, the breeding season falls in the later part of that time span, while in more southern areas wolves breed quite early in the year. Mating in late winter ensures that pups will be born in spring, when the weather is mild and prey is plentiful. A spring birth also means that pups will have many months to grow and become robust before another harsh winter descends.

PAGES 100–101: : A mother wolf cuddles with her offspring. Typically, the alpha pair are the only wolves in the pack to breed, and the pair nearly always produces young each year.

OPPOSITE: In some instances, subordinate wolves also breed. Availability of prey and the stability of the dominance hierarchy help determine whether lower-ranking wolves reproduce. Firmly dominant alpha females discourage other females from breeding with physical attacks, sometimes stressing their subordinates to the point that they fail to go into estrus at all. Alpha wolves may also actively intervene if less dominant wolves attempt to mate.

RIGHT: A female wolf rolls in the snow during estrus, in the late winter mating season. Females are in estrus only for a week or so, and are fertile for just two to five days.

As the mating season approaches, the male wolves of the pack begin to show great interest in the alpha female, sniffing at her and chasing her relentlessly. The alpha male is most aggressive in his attentions, and he asserts his authority over the other male wolves to prevent them from mating with the female. For her part, the alpha female may outright reject suitors other than the alpha male.

During the mating season, the alpha female becomes the most dominant wolf in the pack, a position she maintains while the pups are in the den. Females also become more aggressive toward each other during breeding season. The alpha female will forcefully attack a lower-ranking female who tries to mate with a male. Despite the attacks that take place during the mating season, few serious injuries occur. Tensions are heightened during this sexually charged time, but the pack understands intuitively that the serious injury or death of one member weakens them all.

The alpha pair mates several times over the five to seven days that the female is in estrus. In a position familiar to many of us from observing neighborhood dogs, the male mounts the female from behind. They remain "tied" together in a literal, physical bond, sometimes for twenty or thirty minutes.

During the mating season, the strong emotional bond between the alpha pair becomes even more tightly knit. The two spend most of their time together, and are openly affectionate toward one another, even curling around each other to sleep.

OPPOSITE, BOTTOM: During courtship, the alpha male and female become even more affectionate than usual spending most of their days and nights in each other's company.

BELOW: Mating wolves sometimes spend as much as thirty minutes locked in physical union. Biologists speculate that this allows enough time for the egg to become fertilized, ensuring that no other male will impregnate the female.

RIGHT: A female wolf excavates soft soil to make a new den. Females are very selective when choosing a den site—they prefer elevated sites, which are not only protected from water runoff but may also serve as good lookouts for predators who could harm the pups.

Preparing for the New Arrivals

Once the female is pregnant, she begins her search for a den. Her decision about a den site affects the entire pack, as all the wolves will hunt and rendezvous near the den site for the duration of the breeding season and until the pups are about eight weeks old. Because the site is important to the health of both the pack and the pups, the female chooses carefully. She must find a place that is warm and dry, unlikely to flood, and as far as possible from threats to the pups such as bears, cougars, or humans. The den must also be located where fresh water and prey animals are abundant. Sometimes, the expectant mother decides to prepare more than one den, in case danger threatens and she must move the pups in a hurry.

The pregnant female most often excavates her own den by digging into the soft earth of a hillside. The small opening, big enough for only the female to enter, leads into a narrow tunnel to a chamber where she will bear the pups, and where the young will live for the first month of their lives. She digs the tunnel on an upward slope into the hill, so that water does not run down into the den. Instead of digging her own den, a female may elect to enlarge an existing burrow, such as the deserted den of a fox, or she may den in a cave, a hollow in a tree, or even a simple depression in the ground. Once a female wolf finds a good den, she may use that same site for several years, selecting a different site only once the den has been disturbed or if new threats appear.

OPPOSITE: This wolf mother moves her black phase wolf to a new den. Wolves typically move the pups when a den site is threatened by predators, humans, or weather conditions such as flooding, or if the den becomes contaminated by parasites. When a female moves her pups, she takes the scruff of the pup's neck gently in her teeth, which causes the pup to promptly go limp.

The female gestates for nine weeks, and she may select a site and prepare the den as much as three weeks in advance of the pups' arrival. Once the den is ready the female maintains it with great care until she is ready to give birth. She goes into the den for her labor, usually entering a day or two before the pups are born.

But preparations for the pups' arrival are not confined to the pregnant female. Raising the young is a group effort, and the entire pack awaits the birth of the litter with excitement. As the female prepares the den, other wolves cache food near the site so that she will have nourishment after the pups are born. They also patrol the area carefully, driving away any predators that venture too close to the den site.

The Birth of the Litter

After a gestation period of approximately sixty-three days, the pups are born. The female gives birth alone, and will snarl and snap at an alpha male who tries to enter the den at this time. Birthing an average litter of five pups typically takes about three hours, usually with twenty minutes to an hour between the birth of each pup. After she delivers her offspring, the new mother bites off the umbilical cords that linked the pups to her during their time in the womb, and clears the amniotic sac away by licking the pup vigorously. Once the pups are cleaned up, she helps them find her nipples and they begin to nurse. Wolf milk is vitamin-rich and high in fat, designed by nature to help pups grow quickly.

Litters of four to six pups are by far the most common, but large litters of ten or eleven have been observed, as have litters as small as two or three. The newborn pups are completely helpless, reliant on their mother for food, warmth, and protection. Weighing only one pound (454g) at birth, the pups' do not open their eyes for about two weeks. They cannot hear, maintain their body temperatures, or walk. Instead, they crawl on their stomachs using chiefly their front legs. Although siblings may grow up to be quite different physically, with coats of varying colors and distinctive features, wolf pups look remarkably similar. All are covered with downy, dark brown fur, and have characteristic rounded baby features, with short blunt snouts and floppy ears.

BELOW: Completely helpless at birth, wolf pups have dark, downy fur and rounded, babyish features. Though they are virtually identical as newborns, these littermates may grow up to have different coat colors.

For the first few weeks, their mother is the only adult the pups are exposed to. Her role is that of full-time mother, and she stays in the den with her pups, nursing and tending to them. The mortality rate for wolf pups is estimated at about 60 percent, so the mother wolf does everything possible to see that her pups stay warm, dry, and well fed. Meanwhile, the female's packmates continue to hunt, bringing food back to the den for her. While the pups are so young and vulnerable, the new mother leaves the den only to eat the food the pack brings for her and to drink. A lactating female requires a good supply of fresh water, which is why she is so careful to select a den site that is located near a stream or a pond.

109

ABOVE: A mother rests in the den with her pups. During their first two weeks of life, wolf pups can do little but eat and cry. They prefer to be touching their mother or siblings, and will whimper and crawl toward the warmth of other wolf bodies if they become separated in the den.

OPPOSITE, TOP: When wolf pups are around two weeks of age they begin to develop rapidly. Their motor skills improve and they start to walk steadily. At twelve and fifteen days old their eyes open fully, though their vision will remain poor for several additional weeks.

OPPOSITE, BOTTOM: Pups that are just two to three weeks old are already beginning to romp and play with one another, cultivating strong social bonds that may last for years, and which serve as a model for their relationships with other wolves. Even young pups will begin to play at dominating one another.

ABOVE: A female stands patiently while her pups line up to nurse. Wolf mothers pass antibodies to their pups through their milk, protecting the young against diseases the mother herself is immune to. Once the pups are weaned, they may become vulnerable to certain diseases until they are able to build up their own immunity.

111

When the pups are about two weeks old, they open their eyes. Wolf pups are born with blue eyes, but usually the color changes as the pups get older to shades of brown, deep orange, gold, or green, though some do keep their icy blue eyes. Though their eyes may now be open, their vision is still poor and they cannot distinguish shapes for several more weeks. Shortly after the pups open their eyes, they begin to develop milk teeth and start to walk. By three weeks, the mother begins to wean her pups from a diet of milk, regurgitating partially digested meat for them—a sort of wolf version of baby food. They begin to play inside the den, and before long they are ready to venture outside to greet the adult members of their pack.

BELOW: At three to four weeks, pups begin playing at the entrance of the den. By this time, they are better able to regulate their body temperatures and no longer need the closeness of their mother's body to stay warm.

LEFT: Wolf pups have startlingly blue eyes, which are all the more brilliant in contrast to the dark fur of this black phase pup. As pups age, their eyes typically change color, with a beautiful amber being the most common eye color of adult wolves.

Babies of the Pack

The pups leave the safety of the den for brief periods when they are about three to four weeks old. They are introduced to the pack, and the wolves excitedly welcome the pups by gently nuzzling and licking them. These pups are viewed as babies of the pack, and all will participate in their care. After all, the pack is an extended family, and most of the members are related to the young wolves. Adult wolves help raise the next generation by feeding, "pup sitting," and defending the young. The adults watch for marauding predators who might pose a threat to the pups, and generally look out for the safety of the young wolves.

When the pack goes off to hunt, at least one subordinate wolf will stay behind to look after the pups. After a successful hunt, adults gorge themselves on the kill and then return to the rendezvous site, where the pups are waiting eagerly. As the wolves approach, they make high-pitched squeaking noises to let the pups know that dinner is served. The pups swarm around the adult wolves, gently biting and licking their muzzles, which stimulates regurgitation. Adults disgorge the semisolid food either onto the ground for the pups to eat or directly into the pups' mouths. For healthy growth, pups need two to three times more food per pound (454g) of weight than adult wolves do, and the pack keeps very busy trying to meet the demands of the hungry youngsters.

BELOW: Once the pups are old enough to leave the den, the members of the pack take turns caring for the youngsters. At first, the mother wolf stays near the den, but eventually she rejoins the evening hunt. When a wolf pack leaves the pups to hunt, they appoint a pupsitter, who stays behind to watch over them until the rest of the adults return.

LEFT: After a successful hunt, adults return to the pups and disgorge part of the kill. This regurgitation is stimulated by special begging behavior in the pups, who swarm the adults and lick and nip their muzzles.

BELOW: The partially digested, regurgitated meat serves as a wolf baby food.

Play is an important element in the education of wolf pups. Running, climbing, chewing on sticks, chasing their siblings, and stalking and pouncing on anything that moves occupy a large part of the pups' days. While it may appear that the young wolves are merely enjoying themselves, in fact they are developing valuable skills that will serve them well later in life. As the pups grow up, they will improve their endurance, coordination, balance, and strength through such play.

Playtime is not only essential for a young wolf's physical development, it is also critical for social maturation. Romping together creates a physical closeness between siblings that evolves into an emotional bond, promoting solidarity in the pack. Mock fights with littermates and playing at dominating other pups helps the young wolves learn how to fit into the hierarchy. They are mimicking the behavior they observe in adult pack members and preparing themselves for the day each will take his or her own place in the pack hierarchy or leave to found a new pack.

BELOW: Pups make playthings out of sticks, bones, feathers, leaves, and other objects they find. Using these natural toys, they practice skills like pouncing, which will be helpful later in life when they must hunt small creatures such as mice and lizards.

116

LEFT, TOP: The rough-and-tumble play of wolf pups sometimes mimics the more adult displays of dominance they observe in older pack members. Through wrestling and mock fighting, the young wolves begin to decide the patterns of dominance that will likely follow them throughout their lives.

LEFT, BOTTOM: Tug-of-war with a piece of hide is a popular game. The pulling action these pups practice is the same technique they will one day use at a kill, when they must strip meat from a carcass.

At around six weeks of age, the pups are feeling a bit bolder and venture farther from the den, though the older wolves keep a watchful eye on them, as they are not yet experienced enough to handle encounters with predators. As they wander further afield, the youngsters explore every new thing they encounter, from dandelion puffs and twigs to grasshoppers and birds.

RIGHT: A young wolf explores his world, fascinated by everything he finds. Such a small animal wandering alone is vulnerable to predators such as bears, cougars, and even golden eagles, so adults keep close tabs on the young.

BELOW: Adults are very tolerant of the antics of the pups, even allowing the litter to swarm over them in play.

OPPOSITE: The alpha male nuzzles a pup. All the wolves in the pack treat the pups with great affection.

GROWTH CHART

APPROXIMATE AGE	DEVELOPMENT
2 weeks	Eyes open, milk teeth begin to come in
3 weeks	Hearing begins; pups begin to walk on all four legs
3–4 weeks	Mother begins to wean pups, feed them regurgitated food; pups begin to play around the entrance to the den
8–10 weeks	Pups leave the den permanently and move to the rendezvous site
7 months	Pups leave rendezvous site and travel with the pack; begin to hunt with the adults
2 years	Pups are sexually mature

OPPOSITE: Like babies everywhere, wolf pups need their naps. Pups' days are filled with exploring new places, acquiring new skills, and learning their place in the pack, activities that can be truly exhausting.

ABOVE: Wolves begin to form emotional attachments to the animals around them by about three weeks of age. In the wild, pups bond with their littermates and with adults in the pack, but captive hand-reared wolves also bond with the humans who care for them. It is this willingness to substitute human companions for fellow wolves that led to the domestication of the canine.

RIGHT: A mother and her pup peer over a precipice, into the valley below. Wolves seem to like gazing at the countryside from an elevation.

Adult pack members are generally indulgent with the pups, tolerating their rambunctious behavior and sometimes even romping along with them. The pups pester adult wolves constantly, playfully tugging on the grownups' tails, climbing over their backs, and nipping at them. Occasionally, a beleaguered adult will bare its teeth or growl sternly to put an audacious youngster back in its place, but usually the antics of the pups are looked upon with affection.

After about eight to ten weeks, the pups are old enough to leave the den site and move to the rendezvous site. Life at the rendezvous site, which is usually an acre (0.4ha) or so in size, gives the pups a greater taste of freedom. Here

BELOW: Two eight-week-old wolf pups play peacefully with a couple of saplings. At about eight to ten weeks of age, the youngsters are relocated from the den site to a rendezvous site. Wolves seem to prefer rendezvous sites that are on dry ground but situated near water or boggy areas.

they can range a bit farther but still remain under the protection of the adult wolves. Even when the pack hunts, a subordinate wolf remains behind to watch over the pups. Throughout the summer and into the autumn, the pups continue to explore the world around them and hone their skills by stalking birds, bits of grass, and falling leaves, and by role-playing with their littermates.

As the pups mature, the adults begin to teach them which animal species are potential prey and instruct them in hunting strategies. By autumn, the pups are ready to move with the pack, though the adults alter the pace to accommodate the youngsters. By this time, at seven months old, the pups have also acquired enough skill and knowledge to begin actively hunting with the pack. The pack travels through its territory, searching for prey and stopping occasionally to rest.

By late winter, the pack is ready to begin the cycle of producing new wolves all over again, though the previous litter are still juveniles. Wolves reach physical maturity at about two years of age. While the young wolves may be sexually mature at two, most will not be in a dominant enough position to breed for several more years. After two years, some of the pups leave the pack to become lone wolves, or dispersers, and eventually find a mate and establish new packs. Until then, they travel with their parents, learning to hunt, mark their territories, and fit into the tightly knit society of the wolf pack.

BELOW: An adolescent wolf of unknown age stands beside a packmate. When wolves are about six months old, they look very much like adults, and by ten months of age they are virtually indistinguishable from adult wolves, though the youngsters are not yet sexually mature.

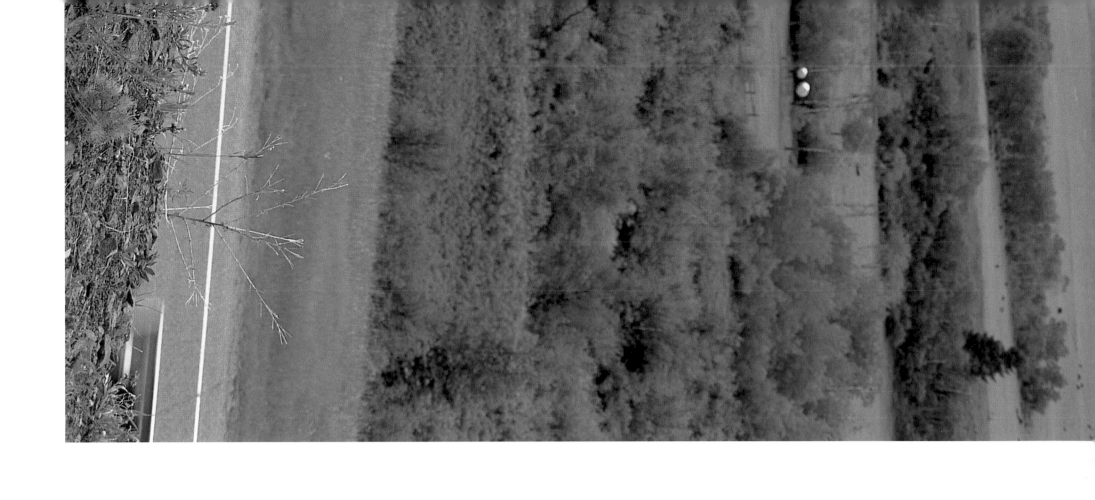

HUMANS
AND
WOLVES

A Troubled History

Negotiating a healthy balance between the needs of modern society and the delicate and complex web of environments that make up our Earth is among the most significant challenges that remains before us. How we solve the ecological dilemmas that confront us has far-reaching ramifications not only for animals and their wild places but ultimately for us humans as well. It is only by committing to the preservation of all wild creatures and their natural homes that we will preserve ourselves, but the road to such a commitment has been long and fraught with perils.

Though early humans had a close enough relationship with wolves to have domesticated some of their number, by the medieval period hatred of wolves had become part of European culture. Nobility and peasantry alike regarded the wolf as a bloodthirsty creature ready to attack at the slightest provocation, and tales of wolves assaulting helpless women and innocent babes abounded. While these stories were no doubt greatly exaggerated, it is not surprising that there was conflict between a surging population struggling to protect its livestock and hungry wolves displaced by ever-increasing tracts of farmland. Wolves are typically shy creatures, but a wolf driven by hunger may become desperate enough to attack people. Past tales of vicious wolf attacks were so numerous that historians and wolf biologists believe that there may be an additional explanation, speculating that wolves could have picked up rabies from dogs, and that these diseased wolves were responsible for the attacks. It is actually exceedingly rare for a wolf to attack a human, and in North America there have been no documented cases of healthy wild wolves killing people.

PAGES 124–125: Wolves are shy animals that avoid people when possible, but encroaching human settlements have made this more difficult. As the wolf's natural prey becomes less available, the animals seek to find other food, sometimes replacing wild ungulates with livestock. Here, a wolf looks out over a Montana ranch.

OPPOSITE: Researchers monitor the numbers and movements of wolves by fitting them with radio collars. Good data on wolf populations helps conservationists formulate effective management plans.

Werewolf lore also doubtlessly fueled the European hatred of wolves. "Eyewitness" accounts of wolves turning into men and vice versa flourished, with many cautionary tales centering around the immoral life led by the incipient werewolf. Giving in to one's bestial nature was one of the ways that a person could purportedly become a werewolf, and thus the wolf became a symbol of evil and sin.

This prejudice against wolves was deeply entrenched by the time Europeans crossed the Atlantic to the New World. Though the vast wilderness of North America should have ensured that the two species would be able to maintain their distance, even the presence of wolves in the vicinity appeared as a menace to the new settlers. Just a decade after the Puritans arrived on the *Mayflower*, the magistrates of Plymouth Colony set a cash bounty on wolves. A few years later the threat from wolves was judged so serious that the bounty was increased to the equivalent of one month's wages. Persecution of wolves continued and grew, as more and more land was cleared for towns and farms, and as settlers of European descent moved ever westward.

Wolves were not only killed because of their perceived threat to humans and livestock. In the mid-nineteenth century, the American consumer developed a preference for the furs of bison, elk, deer, and wolves. In addition to being slaughtered for their own skins, wolves suffered from the significant reduction in large prey available to them.

Pursued relentlessly for more than two hundred years, wolf populations began to decline precipitously. Hunters, trappers, farmers, ranchers, and sportsmen continued to kill these predators with shotguns and steel traps, and by poisoning them with strychnine. Some estimates put the number of wolves exterminated in the latter part of the 1800s as high as two million.

Even the U.S. government joined the fray. Under the aegis of the United States Biological Survey, the government hired hunters and trappers to eradicate the wolf population once and for all. Among the Survey's stated purposes at its founding in 1907 was to rid the country of the scourge of wolves, and this concerted effort by and large succeeded. By the 1930s, few wild wolves remained in the lower forty-eight states.

OPPOSITE. TOP: A wolf lies dead, killed by a motorist, in Superior National Forest in Minnesota. Despite such accidents, Minnesota supports a thriving population of wolves.

OPPOSITE. BOTTOM: Famed wolf biologist David L. Mech with three poached wolves. Despite laws that have protected wolves in many areas, they are sometimes killed illegally by hunters or ranchers. The re-evaluation of the gray wolf's status on the endangered species list, and the animal's downgrading to threatened in 2003 in most states, opens the way for ranchers to legally kill wolves that attack livestock.

128

Steps in the Right Direction

Fortunately for both wolves and humans, attitudes have changed over the past quarter century, and wildlife managers and the public alike now recognize the value of the wolf in helping to maintain a healthy ecosystem. At the time they sought to annihilate the wolf, people did not fully understand this predator's important role in selectively culling herds of wild ungulates. Without an apex predator, populations of wild deer, caribou, moose, and other large hoofed mammals went unchecked, and some of these animals died slow, painful deaths from starvation. In their attempt to find food and stay alive, these large mammals also ravaged the vegetation in their range, sometimes causing serious damage to the environment.

An educated public has also come to appreciate the wolf for its magnificent beauty, its sophisticated social organization, and its history as an integral part of the North American environment. Furthermore, we now recognize that, while a commitment of time, money, and creativity is required, it is possible to find good wildlife management solutions that allow humans and wolves to coexist.

Ironically, one of the earliest attempts to preserve wild animals and places did not protect the wolf, and even served as an agent of annihilation. When the National Park Service was established in 1916, it systematically persecuted wolves and other predators rather than providing relief for them. The philosophy of national parks at that time was that they should be refuges for "peaceful" animals such as deer, elk, moose, and bighorn sheep. In fact, the Park Service desired to keep these grazing herd animals, which drew crowds of tourists, safe from predators such as wolves, mountain lions, coyotes, and eagles. To this end, they maintained the policy of killing any wild predators they found within park limits.

It was not until the Endangered Species Act was passed by Congress in 1973 that serious efforts to preserve the entirety of our wild heritage were launched. The Endangered Species Act is intended to protect any animal threatened with danger of extinction due to habitat destruction, depletion of prey, threats from humans or diseases, or any other factor that might jeopardize the species. Under the act, the penalty for killing a

OPPOSITE: Wolves at Yellowstone National Park hunt elk. Though wolves were native to the area encompassed by the park, they had been largely absent from Yellowstone since the 1940s. In 1991, Congress funded an Environmental Impact Statement that would study the effects of wolf reintroduction to Yellowstone, and in 1995 fourteen wolves were released into the park.

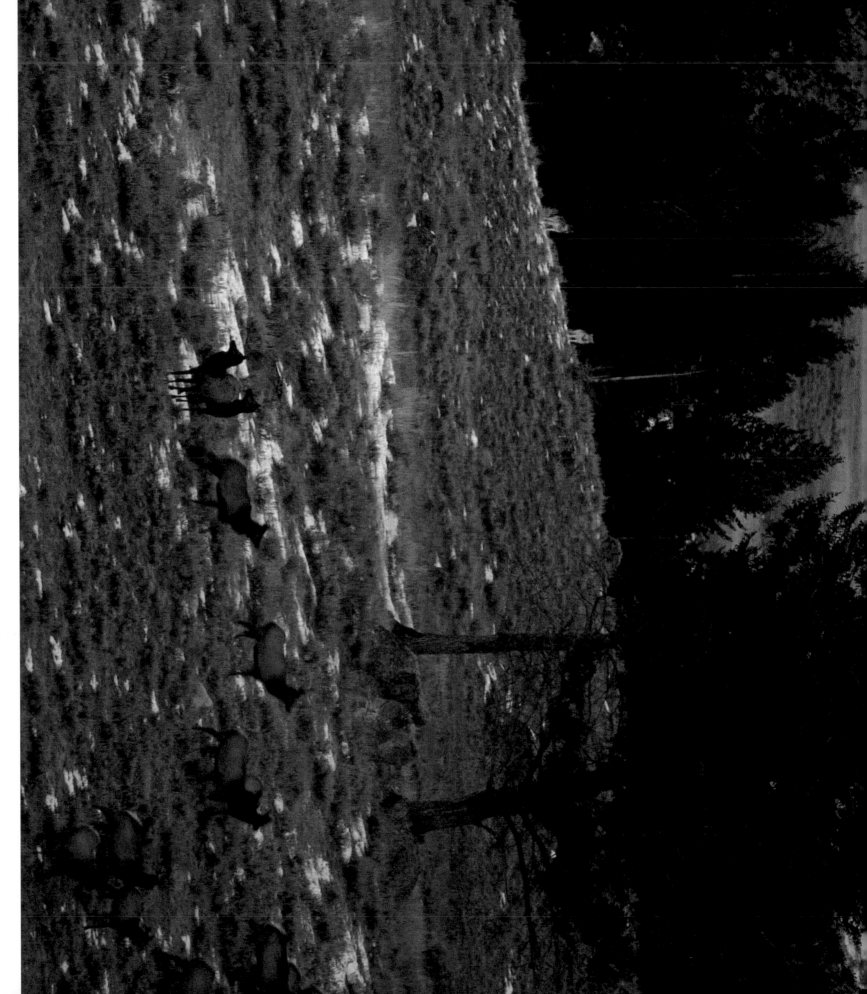

wolf in an area where the animal is designated as endangered is a fine of up to $50,000 and as much as a year in prison. However, some hunters and ranchers continue to defy this federal law, and wolves are still illegally shot, poisoned, and caught in traps.

In March 2003, gray wolves in most of the lower forty-eight states (they had received no special protection in Alaska) were downlisted from "endangered" to "threatened." Alaska; Minnesota; Isle Royale in Lake Superior;

TEMPORARY
AREA CLOSURE

AREA BEYOND THIS POINT CLOSED TO PUBLIC USE AND
TRAVEL FOR THE WOLF REINTRODUCTION PROGRAM
- PURSUANT TO 36 CFR 1.5 (A) 1 -

YOU ARE HERE

NATIONAL PARK SERVICE

UNITED STATES DEPARTMENT OF THE INTERIOR

RIGHT: A sign at Yellowstone indicates the wolves' need for peace and privacy as they acclimate to their new home. Yellowstone's wolves were captured in the Canadian wilderness and relocated to the park. The first fourteen wolves released in Yellowstone produced two litters, totalling nine pups, their initial season, giving conservationists cause for optimism.

OPPOSITE, TOP: Alaska sustains a healthy population of wolves, but even in this state the wolf faces controversy. In some years, declining numbers of caribou spur some people to petition for wolf control programs, though a number of studies suggest that the fluctuating populations are more a factor of cycles in winter weather than wolf predation.

OPPOSITE, BOTTOM: A red wolf gazes through the barbed wire barrier meant to keep the animals inside the Great Smoky Mountains National Park. Red wolves were reintroduced to the park in 1991; however, the wolves failed to establish home ranges within the park and pups suffered extremely high mortality rates, leading to discontinuation of the reintroduction program there.

Michigan's upper peninsula; Yellowstone National Park; and parts of Idaho, Montana, and Wisconsin support wild gray wolf populations, and the open wilderness areas of Canada have long sustained healthy populations of wolves. Mexican wolves have been reintroduced along the Arizona–New Mexico border, and currently live there in small numbers. Red wolves have been reintroduced into North Carolina's Alligator River National Wildlife Refuge and to several islands along the coast of North Carolina. They were also reintroduced to Great Smoky Mountains National Park, though these efforts failed and the program was discontinued.

Managing Wild Wolves

Today, conservationists—from the National Park Service, the U.S. Fish and Wildlife Service, wildlife parks, and private organizations—work together to preserve and manage the wolf in its wild habitat according to principles outlined by the Wolf Specialist Group of the International Union for the Conservation of Nature and Natural Resources (IUCN). These principles are codified in the Manifesto on Wolf Conservation, first drafted in 1973, then revised in 1983, 1996, and 2000. Two separate parts—a Declaration of Principles for Wolf Conservation and Guidelines for Wolf Conservation—comprise the Manifesto, and together they provide a strong foundation for the conservation of wolves and a basic blueprint for the effective management of wolf populations.

The guidelines offer practical advice and solutions, including encouraging compensation for damage caused by wolves through predation, and advocating wolf-related tourist activities where they are appropriate. Tourism can do more than provide education about wolf conservation; wolf-watchers who visit national parks and wild animal refuges spend millions of dollars on hotels, souvenirs, and park fees, providing jobs for the people who live in those areas.

To facilitate reintroduction and management, biologists have developed a number of practical strategies for capturing, examining, acclimating, releasing, and tracking wolves. These practices not only help researchers learn more about wolves and they way they live, the methods also ensure that the wolves have the best possible chance at success after they are reintroduced to the wild.

Wolves who begin to range outside the boundaries of a park or conservation area will be reacclimated to the territory set aside for them. Wolf biologists capture them and return them to the park, often confining them to a reacclimation pen for several weeks before they are rereleased.

Capturing the Wolf

There are any number of reasons that a wild wolf may need to be captured by a researcher. Wolves introduced into the wild in one range are often simply moved from one territory to another (this is technically called translocation rather than reintroduction). The wolves of Yellowstone, for example, were translocated wild wolves from Canada. A wolf may also be translocated if it proves troublesome, for example, leaving its territory to prey on livestock or other domestic animals.

OPPOSITE: An endangered red wolf is removed from a carrier at the Alligator River National Wildlife Refuge. In an experimental reintroduction program begun at Alligator River in 1986, critically endangered red wolves proved that they could adapt to life, and breed successfully, in the wild.

Wolves are also captured so they can be fitted with radio collars, used for tracking. Pups born in the wild must be fitted once they have grown close to their mature size, and some wolves lose their collars. Also, batteries in radio collars stop working after a few years and must be replaced. Finally, a sick or injured wolf may be captured so that it can receive medical attention.

ABOVE: Biologists fit a red wolf with a radio collar before releasing it into the wild at the Alligator River National Wildlife Refuge. Before release, the animal will also be given a thorough physical examination by a veterinarian and vaccinated against disease.

Aerial darting is one method that researchers use to capture wolves in the wild, and a helicopter is the craft of choice for aerial darting. A disadvantage of this method is that the wolves must be in an open area, which is not always possible. The helicopter flies beside the running wolves and a shooter poised in the doorway of the helicopter aims a dart into the rump of the animal they are looking to catch. The helicopter may contact crew on the ground to retrieve the fallen animal, or the aircraft may land to pick up the tranquilized animal.

In areas that are thickly forested, leghold traps are more practical. Modern leghold traps used by wolf researchers are very similar to those previously used to catch and kill wolves, but these newer traps are designed not to injure the wolf. The trap's jaws are locked open, and a wolf attractant is used as bait. When the wolf is drawn to the irresistible scent of the attractant, it triggers a mechanism that causes the jaws snap shut with the wolf's leg secure in the trap.

Once the wolf has been captured, the animal is examined by a veterinarian, weighed, measured, and, if necessary, treated for any medical conditions. If it is to be translocated, the wolf begins its long journey to its new home.

Acclimation

Once the wolf has arrived at its new home, the release program will begin. There are two basic types of releases: the hard release and the soft release. For the hard release, the animal is simply transported in a crate to the site where it is to be introduced and then let go.

LEFT: A wolf is transported from a helicopter to the truck that will take it to an acclimation pen in the heart of its new home. Holding the animals in an acclimation area gives them the best chance for survival, allowing them time to adapt to their new surroundings and to adjust to the taste of the prey available in those environs. Adolescent wolves are ideal candidates for reintroduction because they have not yet established a home range, and are more likely to readily accept their new territory.

The soft release requires that the wolf be kept in an acclimation pen in the territory where it is to be released for several weeks or even for several months. Because the wolf has time to grow used to the sights, sounds, and smells of its new home, this sort of release is less traumatic for the animal. Researchers also hope that a significant amount of time spent in an acclimation pen will reduce the chance that a wolf will head back to its former territory, though some wolves do in fact try to return to their old homes.

It is also possible that the site where a wolf is being introduced is populated with different sorts of prey than it might be used to. Researchers helping to acclimate the wolf will feed it the types of meat it is likely to encounter in its new home.

Acclimation pens are constructed of chain-link fencing, which must be sturdy and well constructed in order to keep the wolves safely inside. Because wolves are fairly good jumpers, fences are at least eight feet high (2.4m) and are built with an overhang to make escape more difficult. There is also a barrier that prevents the wolves from tunneling under the fence.

Humans are the wolf's most dangerous enemy, so during the acclimation period researchers take great care to avoid unnecessary contact with the wolves. It is in the wolf's best interest to maintain a healthy fear of humans, and to keep its distance from houses and farms. Wolves that become habituated to humans may begin to raid garbage cans or camp sites and may approach humans looking for food, even becoming aggressive at times.

Before a wolf is released, researchers will give it a medical examination and will vaccinate it against disease. It will also be weighed and measured and fitted with a radio collar that helps the researchers track the wolf. When the animal is released, the door is simply left open and the animal is free to explore its new surroundings at its own pace.

Radio Tracking

Tracking animals with radio collars, known as radio telemetry, is a well-established practice among wildlife researchers. When a wolf is released into the wild (or after it has been captured in the wild, examined, and rereleased) it is fitted with a radio collar that can track its movements. The collar weighs approximately one pound (454g) and emits a signal at a particular frequency. A researcher tracks the animal's movements by tuning in to the correct frequency and pointing the antenna of the receiver in the direction of the wolf; the researcher then draws a line

OPPOSITE: This radio-collared female gray wolf stalks the edges of a pond, searching for duck nests. Through radio telemetry, researchers can learn how many of the wolves survive, and they can locate a pack to determine whether any members have been born or have dispersed or died.

on a map to represent the direction the signal is coming from. The researcher must then move to another site and track the wolf again; the spot where the second line on the map intersects the first line represents the location of the wolf.

Some sophisticated transmitters can emit different sounds depending upon the activities of the wolf. These more specific signals allow the researcher to learn whether the wolf is running or resting. All transmitters emit a mortality signal, which tells the researcher that the wolf has not moved in a number of hours. In this case, either the animal has died or the collar has come off.

The difficulty with radio telemetry is that the presence of cliffs and hills, and even trees, can interrupt the signal. Also, the receiver must be within about two or three miles of the transmitter for the signal to be readable. This makes tracking on the ground a somewhat inefficient process. Radio tracking by air is much easier, because interference from objects on the ground is less and because you can cover more distance, hopefully picking up more signals. The main difficulty with tracking by air is the expense.

These tools help wolf biologists understand more about their wild subjects, and the better we understand wolves, their needs, and their place in the ecosystem, the better we can protect them. Wolf management programs aim to restore a healthy balance to the ecosystem, and through continued research and public education, wolf conservationists are fighting not only for the future of these magnificent creatures, but for the future of the entire Earth.

Conclusion

Only in the past few decades have humans turned from their long-held hatred of wolves as vicious predators to acknowledge these animals' integral role in a healthy ecosystem and to admire their majestic wild presence. From relentless persecution, which nearly eradicated the wolf across much of North America, we have traveled a long road to appreciation of this creature's ingenuity as a cooperative hunter, adaptability to a changing environment, and loving care of pups and packmates.

Wolf conservation is, in a number of ways, a barometer of the nation's commitment to its natural heritage. Because wolf restoration programs require us to make sacrifices—of land, of money, of time—they challenge us to find ways to balance our own economic needs and our desire for comfort and modernity with the greater good of our wild neighbors. And ultimately, it is only our responsible stewardship of the Earth and its great diversity of creatures that will secure the future of the wolf—and the planet.

LEFT: Understanding and appreciating these handsome creatures is a first step in committing to their preservation. Conservationists and involved citizens dedicated to preserving the wolf and its habitat help ensure that this predator roams the wild not only in our time, but in our children's time, and in their children's time.

Resources

The following organizations maintain websites that provide information about wolves in North America. Some have a strong conservation mission and provide opportunities for activism, while others are primarily educational.

Canadian Centre for Wolf Research
www.wolfca.com

Central Rockies Wolf Project
www.canadianrockies.net/wolf

Eastern Office
R.R. #3
Ailsa Craig, Ontario
Canada N0M 1A0
519–293–3703

Western Office
910–15th Street
Canmore, Alberta
Canada T1W 1X3
403–678–9633

Defenders of Wildlife
www.defenders.org/wildlife/new/wolves
1130 17th St, NW
Washington, DC 20036

International Wolf Center
www.wolf.org
1396 Highway 169
Ely, MN 55731–8129
218–365–4695

North American Wolf Association
www.nawa.org
23214 Tree Bright
Spring, Texas 77373
281–821–4439

Predator Conservation Alliance
www.predatorconservation.org
PO Box 6733
Bozeman, Montana 59771
406–587–3389

Project Wolf
www.projectwolf.org
7600 Waukegan Rd.
Conroe, TX 77306
281–866–8479

Red Wolf Sanctuary
www.redwolf.org
PO Box 235
Dillsboro, IN 47018
812–667–5303

Timber Wolf Information Network
www.timberwolfinformation.org
E110 Emmons Creek Road
Waupaca, WI 54981

Wild Canid Survival & Research Center
at Washington University's
Tyson Research Center
www.wolfsanctuary.org
PO Box 760
Eureka, MO 63025
636–938–5900

Wolf Country
www.wolfcountry.net

Wolf Education and Research Center
www.wolfcenter.org

418 Nez Perce
PO Box 217
Winchester, Idaho 83555
208–924–6960

111 Main Street
Room 150
Lewiston, Idaho 83501
208–743–9554

Wolf Haven International
www.wolfhaven.org
3111 Offut Lake Road
Tenino, WA 98589

Wolf Park
www.wolfpark.org
Battle Ground, IN 47920
765–567–2265

Wolf Web
www.wolfweb.com

Yellowstone Wolf Pack Information Center
www.yellowstone-natl-park.com/wolf.htm

Index

A

Acclimation of wolves, 137,
137–138
Acclimation pen, 138
Aerial darting, 136
Affection, 105, 118, 122
Age, 22
Aggression, 64, 64
Alaska, 133
Alaskan malamute, 10
Alaskan wolf. See Rocky
    Mountain wolf
Alligator River National Wildlife
    Refuge, 132, 135, 136
Alligators, 92, 92
Alpha wolves. See also Leader
    affectionate, 105
    breeding, 100–101, 103–105
    courtship of, 104, 105
    death of, 54–55
    forming packs, 57
    in hierarchy, 51, 52, 52, 54
    scent marking by, 66, 67
Apex predators, 77, 130
Arctic fox, 93
Arctic wolf, 13, 14, 14, 19

B

Barks, 61, 71
Bears, 92, 94, 95
Beaver, 82, 82, 96
Beta wolves
    breeding, 55, 102, 103
    in hierarchy, 51, 52, 53, 55
Biders, 57
Birth, 108
Bison, 81, 82, 82
Black bear, 92
Black phase wolves, 18
Body temperature, 23–24
Bonding, 121
Breathing, 23
Breeding season, 103–105
Buffalo wolf. See Great Plains wolf

C

Canid family, 10–11, 12–13
Canine teeth, 28, 28
Canis dirus, 17
Canis latrans. See Coyotes

Canis lupus. See Gray wolves
Canis lupus arctos. See Arctic wolf
Canis lupus baileyi. See Mexican
    wolf
Canis lupus lycaon. See Eastern
    gray wolf
Canis lupus nubilus. See Great
    Plains wolf
Canis lupus occidentalis. See Rocky
    Mountain wolf
Canis rufus. See Red wolves
Capturing wolves, 134–136
Caribou, 78, 80, 82, 82
Carnassial teeth, 28, 28
Carnivora, 16
Chase games, 71
Claws, 12, 32, 33
Coat, 12
    age and, 22
    of Arctic wolves, 14, 19
    colors of, 18, 22, 22
    of Eastern gray wolves, 14
    of gray wolves, 18, 18–21, 22
    of Great Plains wolves, 14–15
    of Mexican wolves, 15
    of pups, 108, 108
    of red wolves, 38
    of Rocky Mountain wolves, 15
    shaking, 22
    shedding, 23, 23
Communication, 50, 59–67
Conservation of wolves, 130–141
Cougars, 92, 92
Courtship, 104, 105
Coyotes, 93, 93
    interbreeding with gray wolves,
    13, 17, 39

D

Dall sheep, 83, 83
Death
    causes of, 36
    humans and, 128, 131
    of leader, 54–55
Declaration of Principles for
    Wolf Conservation, 134
Deer, 78, 83, 83, 88
Den, 106–107, 106–107
Dew claw, 12, 32, 32
Diet, 82–85, 97–98
Digestion, 87–90

Digitigrade movement, 33
Dire wolf, 17
Dispersers. See Lone wolf
Dogs, 9–12, 10, 11
Domestic animals, as prey, 98

E

Ears, 14, 62
Eastern gray wolf, 12, 13, 14, 14
Eastern timber wolf. See Eastern
    gray wolf
Eating, 87–90, 88, 89
Elk, 76, 84, 84
Endangered Species Act, 130
Endangered species list, 9, 15,
    131–132
Environmental Impact Statement,
    131
Estrus, 103, 104
Evolution of wolves, 16, 16–17
Eye color, 112, 113

F

Facial expressions, 63–65, 64
Feast or famine lifestyle, 86, 87–90
Fighting, 37, 70
    mock, 71, 73, 116, 117
Fish, 97
Foxes, 12, 93, 93
Fur. See also Coat
    layers of, 20, 22

G

Gestures, 62, 62–63
Gray wolves, 6–7, 18–27
    evolution of, 16–17
    interbreeding with coyotes, 13,
    17, 39
    subspecies of, 13, 14–15
    taxonomy of, 12, 13
Great Plains wolf, 13, 14–15
Great Smoky Mountains
    National Park, 132, 133
Greeting, 70, 72
Grizzly bear, 92, 94, 95
Growls, 59, 61, 71
Guard hairs, 22
Guidelines for Wolf
    Conservation, 134

H

Habitat, 40–41
Hair, 22. See also Coat
Hard release, 137
Hearing, 35, 35
Hesperocyon, 16
Hierarchy, 51, 52–53, 59
Howl, 8, 60, 60–61, 61
Humans
    contact with, 98
    and dogs, 10–11
    hunting wolves, 36, 128, 131
    and wolves, 9, 11, 40–41,
    124–141
Hunting by wolves, 74–99. See
    also Prey
    cooperative, 78–81
    pups learning, 123
Hunting of wolves, 36, 128, 131

I

Ice, 23
Incisors, 28, 28
Interbreeding, among gray wolves
    and coyotes, 13, 17, 39
International Union for the
    Conservation of Nature and
    Natural Resources (IUCN),
    134

J

Jacobsen's organs, 35
Jaw, 29, 29, 87

L

Leader, 24, 25, 46. See also Alpha
    wolves
Leghold traps, 136
Legs, 12, 24
Leptocyon, 16
Linnaeus, Carolus, 12, 18
Litter, 108–112, 108–113
Liver, 90
Livestock, 98
Lobo. See Mexican wolf
Lone wolf, 36, 58, 58, 123

M

Mackenzie Valley wolf. See Rocky
    Mountain wolf
Management of wolves, 130–141

Manifesto on Wolf Conservation, 134
Mating, 103–105
Mech, David L., 68, 129
Mexican wolf, 13, 15, 15, 40
Miacidae, 16
Miacis, 16, 16
Milk, 108, 111
Mock fighting, 71, 73, 116, 117
Molars, 28, 28, 87
Molting, 23, 23
Monogamy, 57, 103
Mood, 62, 63
Moose, 78, 81, 84, 84, 87
Mortality signal, 139
Mountain goat, 85, 85
Musk ox, 85, 85
Muzzles, 12
  of Arctic wolves, 14
  and facial expressions, 64
  grasping, in greeting, 70, 72
  pups nipping, 114, 115

N
National Park Service, 130, 134
Nips, 59, 71
Non-retractable claws, 12, 32
Nursing, 108, 111

O
Omega wolves
  abuse of, 70
  in hierarchy, 51, 52, 53, 53, 55

P
Pack, 46–57
  communication in, 50, 59–67
  eating, 87, 88, 89
  forming, 57
  hierarchy of, 51, 52–53, 59
  hunting, 78–81
  politics of, 68–70
  raising pups, 107, 114–122
  size of, 47, 97
Pancreas, 90
Patrolling territory, 34, 67
Paws, 12, 29–33, 32, 33
Plantigrade movement, 33
Play, 71, 71, 112, 116, 116, 122
Poaching, 129
Posture, 59, 62, 62–63, 68
Pregnancy, 107
Premolars, 28, 28
Prey, 77–85. See also specific prey
  of Arctic wolves, 15

domestic animals as, 98
of Great Plains wolves, 15
of Mexican wolves, 15
of red wolves, 39
of Rocky Mountain wolves, 15
  small, 96–98
Pups, 100–123
  birth of, 108
  bonding, 121
  coat of, 108, 108
  growth and development of,
    109–112, 109–113, 120
  in hierarchy, 51, 52, 53, 53, 57
  learning to hunt, 123
  pack raising, 107, 114–122
  playing, 71, 112, 116, 116, 122
  preparing for, 106–107
  sleeping, 120
  waiting at rendezvous site, 78,
    122, 122–123

R
Radio collars, 126, 135, 136,
    138–139, 139
Red fox, 93
Red wolves, 38, 38–39
  capturing, 135
  evolution of, 17
  with radio collar, 136
  reintroducing, 132, 133
  taxonomy of, 13
Regurgitated food, 112, 114, 115
Reintroduction of wolves, 131,
    132, 133, 134, 135
Rendezvous site, 78, 106, 122,
    122–123
Reproduction. See Mating; Pups
"Riding up," 68
Rocky Mountain wolf, 13, 15, 15
Running, 16, 17, 24, 29–33

S
Scent glands, 66, 67
Scent marking, 34, 66, 67, 67
Senses, 34–35
Shedding, 23, 23
Silver wolves. See Gray wolves
Single file travel, 24, 25
Sleeping, 120
Smell, 34, 34–35
Snarls, 61, 68
Snowshoe hare, 96
Society, wolf. See Pack
Soft release, 138
Squeaks, 61

Squeals, 61
Stare, 68
Stomach, 86
Submission. See Subordinate wolves
Subordinate wolves
  behavior of, 54–56, 59, 62, 62,
    68–69, 69
  in hierarchy, 51, 52, 53, 55
  raising pups, 114
Subspecies of wolves, 13, 14–15
Sweat glands, 23

T
Tails, 12, 62
Taxonomy of wolves, 12–13
Teeth, 12, 28, 28–29, 87
Territory, 34, 40–41, 67
Timber wolves. See Gray wolves
Toes, 32–33, 33
Translocation of wolves, 134
Traveling, 24, 25, 30–31, 33
Trot, 30–31, 33
Tug-of-war, 72, 117
Tundra wolves. See Gray wolves

U
Underfur, 20, 22
United States Biological Survey, 128
Uremic poisoning, 90
Urocyon, 16
U.S. Fish and Wildlife Service, 134

V
Vision, 35, 35
Vulpes, 12, 16. See also Foxes

W
Water, 90
Werewolf, 128
Whimpers, 61
Whines, 61
Wolf milk, 108, 111
Wolverines, 93, 93
Wrestling, 117

Y
Yellowstone National Park, 131, 132

Photography Credits